D0948207

THE
PENNY
CAPITALIST

THE PENNY CAPITALIST

How to Build a Small Fortune from Next to Nothing

ALGERNON HORATIO

ARLINGTON HOUSE·PUBLISHERS
NEW ROCHELLE, NEW YORK

The Wizard of Id and B.C. appear here by permission of Johnny Hart and Field Enterprises, Inc. Reprinted from *The King Is a Fink*, copyright © 1964, 1965 by Publishers Newspaper Syndicate, copyright © 1969 by Fawcett Publications, Inc.; *Remember the Golden Rule*, copyright © 1967 by Publishers Newspaper Syndicate, copyright © 1971 by Fawcett Publications, Inc.; *The Wizard of Id— Yield*, copyright © 1968, 1969 by Publishers Newspaper Syndicate, copyright © 1974 by Fawcett Publications, Inc.; and *B.C. Is Alive and Well!*, copyright © 1964, 1965 by Publishers Newspaper Syndicate, copyright © 1969 by Fawcett Publications, Inc. / Pogo and friends appear here by permission of Simon & Schuster, a Division of Gulf & Western Corporation. Reprinted from *The Pogo Papers*, copyright © 1953 by Walt Kelly; and *Pogo Revisited*, copyright © 1974 by Walt Kelly. / The cartoon on pp. 194–95 is reprinted from *Mad*, copyright © 1976 by E. C. Publications, Inc. / The graphs on pp. 178–79 are from *Money and Art* by Geraldine Keen, copyright © 1971 by Geraldine Keen. Reprinted by permission of G. P. Putnam's Sons. / The quotation on pp. 17–18 is from *How to Reap Riches from Raw Land* by Glen Nicely, copyright © 1974 by Prentice-Hall, Inc. Reprinted by permission of Prentice-Hall, Inc. / The quotation on pp. 66–67 is from *The Intelligent Investor*, 4th rev. ed., by Benjamin Graham, copyright © 1973 by Harper & Row, Publishers, Inc. Reprinted by permission of the publisher. / The table on pp. 74–75 is from *Anyone Can Still Make a Million* by Morton Schulman, copyright © 1972 by McGraw-Hill Ryerson Limited. Reprinted by permission of Bantam Books, Inc. / The quotation on pp. 76–78 is from *How to Manage Your Money: A Woman's Guide to Investing* by Elizabeth M. Fowler, copyright © 1973 by Elizabeth M. Fowler. Reprinted by permission of Little, Brown & Company. / The data in the table on p. 116 is from *Anyone Can Make a Million* by Morton Schulman, copyright © 1971 by Morton Schulman. Reprinted by permission of McGraw-Hill Ryerson Limited. / The quotation on pp. 124–25 is from *Why Most Investors Are Mostly Wrong Most of the Time* by W. X. Scheinman, copyright © 1970 by W. X. Scheinman. Reprinted by permission of the David McKay Company, Inc. / The tables on p. 149 are from *The Rape of the Taxpayer* by Philip M. Stern, copyright © 1972, 1973 by Philip M. Stern. Reprinted by permission of Random House, Inc.

Manufactured in the United States of America

P 10 9 8 7 6 5 4 3 2 1

Book design by Pat Slesarchik

Library of Congress Cataloging in Publication Data

Horatio, Algernon (pseud.)
  The penny capitalist.

  Bibliography: p.
  Includes index.
  1. Investments. 2. Finance, Personal. I. Title.
HG4521.H554   332'.024   78-10256
ISBN 0-87000-422-0

Contents

Preface

I decided to write this book as a result of shopping for an apartment building. Within the past year I considered the purchase of a thirty-unit apartment house. Even though I didn't have the money to buy, I was seriously considering how I could put such a deal together. You may ask *how* I could contemplate buying if I didn't have any money. In reply, I must ask you to read further in order to learn how, but these thoughts led me to realize that if I could indeed contemplate the purchase of a $400,000 building, then I was no longer a "Penny Capitalist" but had advanced, perhaps, to the nickel level. In any event, I believe the techniques that have worked for me can work for others, and it is with this in mind that these suggestions are presented.

The goal of this book is to present a set of concepts and practices that if applied can lead to the acquisition of a nest egg of invested capital. In contrast to most books on investments, then, the primary emphasis is not how to invest, but how to acquire the necessary capital in order to begin an investment program. *The Penny Capitalist* is aimed at the average middle American who runs out of money on the twenty-fifth of every month, has no savings account, and doesn't know where the money is coming from to get his daughter's teeth straightened. Every other book on investments I know of assumes you have from $10,000 to $100,000 lying around and that you need the author's advice on what to do with it. If you are like most of us and have zilch, what have you got to lose by reading this book? If you can follow these suggestions, you may not get

9

rich, but you should be able to build up that first pot of investable capital.

Why bother to build up any capital? I believe W. M. Kiplinger has expressed the reasons as well as anyone (Hazard and Coit 1962, pp. 15–16):*

> Another startling discovery, which I made a little late in life, is that money isn't merely money, it isn't just something that you can spend for things you want. It's more than that: it's one of the products of years of work. It's the surplus energy of a lifetime. It's a helper, a servant that will work for you while you are doing your own work, whatever that is. It's a college education for someone. It's a trip to Europe. It's a life-saver in emergencies, for you, or members of your family, or friends, either close or distant. It's a way of giving them of yourself, for money is a sort of distillation of yourself—or it can be if you manage right.
>
> Or another thing you can do with money is to give it away as you think best—to persons or to causes— and have for yourself the internal pleasure of seeing it brighten a number of situations. You can watch the growth of the benefits just as you have watched the growth of the money itself. Fun at both ends of the deal, a double bargain in human values, like a hobby, a profitable hobby.
>
> I learned also that just as people grow with time and experience, and become bigger, better and more useful persons, so money can grow and become a useful partner. These two good partners, working together instead of just one lone individual, accomplish *much* more. Previously I had looked upon money (when I looked upon it at all) as something cold and earthy and perhaps a bit sordid, certainly not to be associated with the finer things of life. But gradually I came to see that money is one of the givers of whatever you want in life, fine or otherwise, selfish or otherwise. Not an end in itself, but a means to all sorts of ends.

---

* For a full citation see References, pp. 239–40.

The Golden Rule

If Kiplinger's views didn't perk up your interest, perhaps the accompanying observation from "The Wizard of Id" did!

At this point you may be wondering how I have fared following my own advice. I can tell you that my family's net worth has increased ten times in the last nine years. Even with a cumulative inflation rate of 64 percent, that still leaves a net capital growth of 936 percent. Please note that if we cashed in now we would be liable for capital gains taxes, so our net would be somewhat reduced, probably to about the 700 percent level.

Throughout this book I have related the exploits in offbeat investing of a number of my friends and acquaintances. These individuals, the Fastest Trader in the West, the Basket Man *et al.*, really exist, and their adventures are truthfully related. Others, the Antique Lady and the Inheritor, are composites of several individuals. However, their activities are also faithfully presented. The Apartment Pyramider, who herein does splendidly at every turn, got caught with a high vacancy rate and high monthly payments in 1977 and was foreclosed. He is back selling real estate now, but I predict he will be buying equities again in the near future.

As far as my own exploits in investing are concerned, I have provided a highly personalized account. This is not a book that discusses the advantages of each type of investment in a neutral or objective manner. I have described both those investments that worked well for me and those that, for a number of reasons, didn't work out so well. The latter forms of investment may work well for others, but where they didn't pan out for me, I say so and attempt to explain why.

After reading this book, you should be better prepared to go forth and do battle against the forces that make it so difficult for anyone to accumulate capital these days. All of the principles explained herein are valid for today's conditions. They are highly tuned to a state of continuing inflation, and it is with an expectation that inflation will continue for the foreseeable future that this investment approach is offered. I hope these rules for action will work as well for you as they have for me.

1

Introduction

How often have you read a magazine article that proclaimed some panacea such as "1001 Ways to Stretch the Family Budget," or "New Recipes for Cheaper Cuts of Meat," or "How I Fed a Family of Eight on $30 Per Week," or "Shopping Hints for the Pennywise"?

The one thing all such articles have in common is that they suggest conservative budgeting will lead to a contented and secure future for you and your family. According to these authorities, this approach will provide extra funds that can be invested to provide for tomorrow, and at the same time make it possible for you to meet all your current needs. It sounds good, and it may work for some, but if these articles are in fact so helpful, why do they appear with such frequency? One might suspect that either these techniques aren't all they are cracked up to be or there are other underlying causes that act to prevent this glowing vision of financial security from becoming a reality.

Several causes seem to me to be important. The first of these is that no one really wants to live on his present income. The second is the inability of many to distinguish between wants and needs. The third is inflation. If you're still counting, you can also throw in taxes.

Of these problems, the most important to resolve is the first. If you don't like your present income, what can you do about it? Here is where all the good budgeting advice I have read fails. The concept that is normally unquestioned is that one's income, whatever it may be, is adequate if properly managed.

Well, maybe so. But owing in part to our tax structure, that seems to me unlikely. At least 90 percent of all families have incomes they would term inadequate. These inadequacies take many forms, but normally include insufficient savings to meet emergencies, inadequate housing, inadequate insurance, inadequate provision for retirement income, and insufficient funds for recreation. Common "remedies" include nonpayment of bills, postponing what's needed, and doing without altogether. The long anticipated raise is spent before it's received, and when it arrives, inflation and taxes have already given it a good clobbering.

How then can you proceed to the next level, that of satisfying your wants, when even your needs aren't being met? The budgeting savants concede very little to the satisfaction of your wants; after all, in their view what is needed is restraint in spending in order to achieve the perfect harmony of a balanced budget.

I disagree. After all, what do you live for if not to satisfy some of your wants? The healthy family budget, it seems to me, must include something that is spent for the sheer joy of it, indulging hobbies, or palate, or whatever makes you feel that life is indeed worth living. What is needed is a method to increase the usable portion of your income to include both needs and wants.

A further consideration is the building of a nest egg for the future. At this point another set of conditioned savants pops up—the investment writers. If you have been so frugal as to save a few thousand dollars, what do you do with it? Their advice is shrouded in mystic jargon, and you read chapters with such exciting titles as "Convertible Bonds" and "Growth versus Income." The standard investment book assumes that, if you are familiar with the various forms of investment, you will make the correct investment decisions. What the usual investment writer often fails to provide is a definition of what an investment is or how you can relate investment decisions to the other day-to-day financial decisions you have to make.

I am further put off by the incredible snobbery that permeates the investment literature. I have learned, for example, that no investment counselor will provide personal guidance if the fund to be invested is so small as $15,000. For such a paltry sum the advice is to buy a mutual fund. I doubt that a mutual fund is your best vehicle if your goal is to build equity for the future. In fact, the recent analytical literature reports that for the 1960s and '70s the average mutual fund didn't even do as well as the Dow Jones stock averages (and for that kind of performance they charge a management fee!). If you have limited funds, you are going to have to go it on your own, making your own decisions, taking the necessary risks, and, if you are right, reaping the rewards. This is the course of action that I have followed, and my decisions have been based on my own "Penny Capitalist" philosophy. It has worked well for me and it is in the hope that these concepts can work for you that they are presented here.

To sum up the goals established so far, you need: (1) to adequately provide for your daily financial needs, (2) to adequately satisfy some of your wants so that you can avoid the psychological problems associated with excessive wish postponement, and (3) to simultaneously place a portion of your income into small investments that will grow into the nucleus of financial security.

Now that the goals are defined, I can outline the methods that will satisfy them.

What Is an Investment?

In order for you to follow any advice I offer, you have to understand what I am referring to when I use terms like *investment, equity,* etc. I seldom use these terms in their standard dictionary senses. My usages are part of my overall investment philosophy, so it is imperative that we understand each other from the very beginning.

The term *investment* is one of the most abused words in the English language; practically everything has been termed an investment at one time or another. Is it an investment to buy a new car, a new dress, a washing machine, shares of Bell Telephone, New York City bonds, Czarist bonds, a percentage interest in a breeding bull, Scotch whiskey, or any other of the thousands of items that you could buy? If these don't suffice, can we include General Motors, IBM, Xerox, or Coca-Cola? What about Sky Blue Pink Ranchettes in Arizona, or a condominium in Vail, or a remote sliver of beach in the Bahamas?

By now you may be getting the idea that the definition of an

15

investment has nothing to do with *what* you buy, but rather what happens after you buy it, and only that. If so, you're right. An investment is the end product of a process that results in an increase in price. If you buy something and the price goes up, it was an investment. If the price goes down, it was not an investment.

Some value may be assigned to the use you get from an item during the time that you own it, but this does not negate the fact that an increase in price must occur for the item to qualify as an investment. Use-value can more properly be budgeted either as a cost to be written off against the realized return or as a fringe benefit that, while not returning income or adding to equity, may have provided you pleasure or saved you from expenditures that you would otherwise have made. A case in point is our ranch. By virtue of the fact that we own pasture and hay land, we also achieve a measure of privacy. Our land isolates us from living too close to our neighbors. It is almost impossible to assign a dollar value to this privacy, but it is a satisfying experience, and we value it all the more because of the years we spent living in a trailer court with a neighbor eight feet away whom we could watch, whether we wanted to or not, frying potatoes while dressed only in a slip.

Utilizing our definition of an investment, we can say that buying a new car or anything else that depreciates in value is not making an investment. You are buying a convenience or a necessary item that may cut your expenses. But if you sell it for less than you paid for it, it is more properly called a consumer item or living expense than an investment.

This brings us to another threshold of understanding: the difference between investment and speculation. Classically, in the investment literature, these two terms are given different meanings. An "investment" is any commitment of funds for the purpose of making a profit with a nominal amount of associated risk. A "speculation" is any such commitment of funds that entails considerable risk. The expectations associated with these two types of commitments differ as well; a greater return is hoped for the speculation in order to balance out the greater risk to one's capital.

Looking at these distinctions from another perspective, the only thing that really counts is what happens over a period of time. The best investment then is one that returns the greatest increase in value over a stated term. In terms of the classical definitions, we can have successful or unsuccessful investments as well as successful or unsuccessful speculations. Benjamin Graham (1973, p. 1) argues that "an investment operation is one which, upon thorough analysis promises safety of principal and an adequate return—operations not meeting these requirements are speculative."

Glen Nicely (1974, pp. 9–11) presents a series of distinctions or characteristics of the speculator versus the investor:

Speculator
1. A speculator considers income from property a by-product.
2. A speculator expects to own property for a relatively short duration—usually less than five years.
3. A speculator uses greater leverage and less equity than an investor.
4. A speculator often uses options instead of ownership to hold property for appreciation.
5. A speculator usually (but not always) concentrates on unimproved property.
6. A speculator acquires property with the primary aim of reselling for profit.
7. A speculator attempts to buy property in the early stages of transition.
8. A speculator often purchases property on which accurate appraisal, based on comparable sales, would be difficult—relying heavily on his own judgment as to both present and future value.
9. A speculator creates a market in slack times—off years. He helps average out brokerage business—some brokers will admit that 10 to 20 per cent, and sometimes higher amounts, of their sales are made to speculators. In the auction business 50 per cent to 75 per cent of the purchases are by speculators.
10. A speculator is often an idea man. He must be resourceful in arriving at a use for property— often a use never thought of by the owner from whom he purchased it.

Investor

1. An investor is one who contemplates holding property for long durations.
2. An investor deals chiefly in income-producing property.
3. An investor usually gets the highest possible monthly or annual return.
4. An investor's aim is usually to pay fully for his property as rapidly as possible—whereas the speculator often expects to sell his equity for a profit.
5. His purpose in acquiring property is sometimes to create an income producing estate for his heirs.
6. An investor usually acquires property with a specific use in mind. The investor's greatest weakness is often in becoming too inflexible. While his risk may be generally less than a speculator—it may be greater. For example, property held in trust for a long period of time may suffer from a decaying neighborhood and if it is downtown property it is extremely vulnerable to value erosion brought about by sprawling subdivisions followed by large shopping malls.

At this point you are probably confused. Let's return to Graham's definition of investment. It has several major emphases: thorough analysis, safety of principal, and adequate return. Each of these areas of concern is fraught with pitfalls for the passive or cautious investor.

The analysis (such as that offered by a brokerage firm or investment counseling service), over a period of time, may be proven to have been inadequate in spite of the reputation of the firm or any endorsements as to the quality or integrity of the analysts. Over the long term, it is a rule of thumb that the greatest mistakes are the result of conservative policies carried out in the face of changing conditions.

Safety of principal is another goal. The simple repayment of dollars invested plus interest is not any guarantee that the principal has not been severely eroded. This is why U.S. Savings Bonds have been such a poor investment. Our government has increased the national debt, increased taxes, gone off a monetary standard that backs our currency with anything of real value, devalued the currency, and simply printed more paper to repay its trusting creditors, the American people. Meanwhile the government's inflationary action of creating more paper money has led to the result that the repaid dollars will buy less than those that were invested. So to put meaning into this goal, we have to recognize that safety of principal includes more than simple repayment of currency; it also must include maintenance of buying power.

The goal of getting an adequate return is subject to the same inherent problems. Therefore what constitutes an adequate return can only be computed after the reduction in buying power resulting from increased taxes and inflation is taken into consideration.

In his bestselling book *The Battle for Investment Survival*, Gerald M. Loeb contends that investing for a modest gain with an associated modest risk is self-defeating. His prescription for the successful investor is to attempt to acquire the maximum gain because if you don't reach that goal you may still be able to realize a profit. Meanwhile, the modest investor may have learned to his dismay that his supposedly secure investment had hidden flaws that permitted the profits to leak away without his knowledge, and he may end up with a loser on his hands.

We come back, then, to the fact that investment appraisals can only be made after the fact. If what you bought increased in price then it was a good investment; if not then it wasn't. What were viewed at the onset as the associated risk factors may or may not have been proven out. Any number of things could have changed the basic factors along the way: inflation, taxes, an oil embargo, etc. When this happens, the entire situation may be restructured and what was an investment in classical terms becomes a loser, and what was initially termed a speculation has been moved to the investment category. Viewed in this way the standard distinctions between investments and speculations seem to me to be largely invalid. The only thing that counts is what happened through time. This has been es-

19

pecially true in recent years with so called investments and tax shelters. Investments have suffered from the frequently hidden diseases of inflation, currency devaluation, high interest rates, low liquidity, increased commissions, and the nondelivery of securities.

What I am proposing is that you dispense with the classical terminology, as it tends to structure your thinking into categories. In the fast-moving present any thinking in prestructured categories is liable to set you up for a loss. Don't listen to the mutual fund salesman who talks about past performances either, as what *has* happened may not happen again. What is required is that you develop your aptitude for spotting those situations that are likely to develop into investments, and those that are likely to bomb. The art of investing is primarily one of predicting the future, and those who rely too heavily on data from the past are going to come out on the short end. If you can predict the future well, all of your speculations will turn into investments.

While I am on the subject, let me also distinguish between investments and tax shelters. A *tax shelter* is a provision of the income tax laws that permits you to reduce the taxes you would normally pay on your income by the amount that is "sheltered." Such shelters include rapid depreciation, investment credits, depletion allowances, well-drilling costs, deductions for interest paid, deferral of income to a later tax year, etc. All tax-shelter provisions are keyed to specific situations, and they were made part of the tax code by Congress to "stimulate the economy" or to satisfy various special interests, from middle-income homeowners to giant oil companies. Such shelters are legal, and they are not necessarily immoral. In fact, it is your duty to yourself as an independent financier to take advantage of them whenever possible to reduce your tax burden.

I will not discuss such shelters further here; chapter 9 deals with the effects of taxation. What needs to be discussed now is the fact that tax shelters have been confused with investments. If you can shelter some of your income from taxation, you can expect a tax reduction or rebate. This differs from a return on an investment. For example, if you are in a 50 percent tax bracket and put $10,000 into an oil-well drilling scheme, the Feds will give you a tax credit of 50 percent of your $10,000. If you end up with a dry hole, it still costs you $5,000. You have had the action of "being in the oil business," which may be worth a few points on the cocktail circuit. You also had a chance of striking oil, which, if it had happened, would have provided you with income on which you would have had to pay tax minus the 22.5 percent depletion allowance.

An even better example is cattle feeding. All you have to do is buy some steers and feed in this tax year and you will get a current-year tax deduction. Next year you sell the steers and get your money back. Meanwhile, you have postponed paying the tax on your income from this year to next. It sounds good, especially if you have an unusually high income this year. But in 1974 and 1975 the cattle market went to pot; those sure-thing limited partnerships in cattle feeding ended up in bankruptcy court; and the temporary losses taken for tax purposes became permanent. (Not just to make the tax-shelter boys feel better, but a lot of lifetime cattlemen went belly-up too, which I guess goes to show the equality of our democratic economy in action.)

The point of all of this is that if you want to invest, invest. If you want a tax shelter, find one. But don't confuse one for the other. Investments have to stand on their own merits. Tax advantages are frequently tied to investments, but they should be kept clearly separate, as they are not basic to the health of investments as a whole, but rather are fringe benefits. After all, the tax savings you effect depend upon your other income, so what looks great to someone else probably has no relevance to you. Remember, your difficulties begin with an inadequate income, not a tax problem.

Wholesale versus Retail

We have another terminological hurdle to get past before we can begin to discuss the Penny Capitalist investment philosophy. *Wholesale* and *retail* are two terms that you absolutely have to understand if you are to make any financial progress. How many times have you bought something from someone who said, "I can get it for you wholesale," and felt that you had made a very good deal? Well, normally the person doing the selling has some motive, usually a sales commission. If he received a commission, then you didn't get it wholesale; you paid something higher than wholesale.

Retail is the other confusing term. We are all familiar with list price, which is on the high end of things and is usually discounted. So the retail price becomes a price somewhat lower than list price. And "wholesale" and "retail" prices are actually closer together than you originally thought. How can you detect the difference and buy at wholesale more often? The rule I use is: If it is a price anyone can recognize as a good deal, it's wholesale. If it is a price that only a fool loaded with money who is in a hurry will pay, then it's retail. Or to turn it around, if you have something you wish to sell quickly, keep pricing it lower (with adequate advertising) until you find a buyer. Probably the final selling price is pretty close to the wholesale level. If you want to get a retail price, you can expect to wait longer and to make more contacts before you make the sale. The key to successful investing, then, is to buy at wholesale prices or below and sell at retail prices or above.

There is another pricing range that is interesting. The Indian jewelry market, for example, has a jobber's price, which is for items sold in quantity to dealers. Wholesale price is offered on individual items in either fast-turnover situations such as pawnshops or dealers' shows. The wholesale price is the average price dealers charge each other on individual items, and includes a 20 percent markup above the jobber's price. Retail price is the price the items are marked for resale in a store, and that price includes an average markup of 100 percent over wholesale price. This pricing provides some price flexibility in the selling, which means that the actual sale price may be 10 to 20 percent less than the marked retail price, permitting the dealer to recover 60 to 80 percent profit. So when you see an ad saying "All Indian Jewelry 50% Off," the dealer may still be making a profit.

Finally, the best of all investment advice is: Buy at a price *below* wholesale. If you can do this, you can always sell to someone at the wholesale price and still show a profit. It sounds difficult, but there are lots of ways to buy at a cost below wholesale. The rewards make it worth your time to learn these methods and to apply them in your search for investment opportunities.

Real Value

One term alone stipulates the difference between good investments and poor ones, and that term is *real value*. Real value is
the only reason why you should buy anything. If you remember
that most investments are either objects, such as paintings and
land, or pieces of paper purporting to represent something of
value then you can see that the only thing you should be interested in are the evidences of real value. The world is full of
things that are less than they seem, and huge industries have
been built on simulated value. That is why we have veneered
furniture, silverplate, cupro-nickel coins, and the American car
that supposedly looks and rides like a Mercedes but costs half
as much. Who's kidding whom? If these things are just as good
as the real McCoy, the action of the marketplace will shift their
prices until they cost just as much. In your search for investments look for the *real value*. If it is there, the workings of the
marketplace over time will usually support your appraisal by
yielding a handsome profit.

Most people cannot see value independent of an endorsement; they cannot distinguish things of value unless someone
tells them which characteristics are indicative of value. Often
the person doing the explaining is only interested in selling
something, and his appraisal is appropriately biased. To give
an example, I recently bought an antique souvenir plate at a
flea market. The plate was covered with dingy gold paint, but
I thought it was a quality product because it had an embossed
design and a maker's mark. Also, I could see what appeared to
be brass showing through in places where the paint was
chipped off. At a dollar, the price seemed to be more than right,
so I bought it. The seller said, "You know it isn't brass," and
I said, "I'll buy it anyway." At home it took only a couple of
minutes with paint remover to reveal the plate to be an English
brass souvenir worth ten times what I paid for it! The point is
that I saw the real value, while the seller didn't; furthermore,
I made the investment in the face of a negative opinion. The
value has to be there for you to make good investments.

I have sold things of inferior quality for more than I paid for
them, but these weren't good investments because the risk of
being unable to find someone to unload them on was too great.

It is also a fact that many people are willing to be fooled if the price discount is great enough. They will pay half to two thirds of the price of the real thing for the simulated item. However, your risks as an investor increase dramatically if the real value isn't there. For example, I bought a modern print on canvas of a Frederick Remington painting for twelve dollars; I sold it at auction for forty. The buyer thought it was an original oil painting and told another dealer that he planned to price it at $300. He made a poor investment because: (1) the item was not what he thought it was—the real value wasn't there—and (2) he didn't know the market. If he had known the market, he would have known that a Remington original was worth about $20,000. From my perspective, in at twelve dollars, out at forty, it made sense. From his point of view, it may have worked out—he may have found a bigger fool to sell to—but the price he paid exceeded the real value, and for all I know he may still be stuck with it.

The way to determine real value is to look for fine workmanship, utility, high-quality materials, artistic quality, and rarity. Items with these attributes have real value. Items made of cheap materials and mass produced by machines don't, and never will.

Price Flexibility

Price flexibility is the mechanism that permits you to make a sale at a profit. If you buy at the market price, the market has to move up before you can find any buyers. However, if you buy at a discount or below wholesale, then you have built-in price flexibility. You can even sell below the average market price and still show a profit. People who buy with price flexibility in mind make money. Those who don't, have their shelves stocked with goods priced so high they can't find any buyers.

The Time/Cost Equation

Any investment must be calculated against the amount of time that it takes to realize an increase in price. For example, the Antique Lady bought an expensive glass vase for $450 and sold it three days later for $500. Her profit was 11 percent figured on the amount invested. However, if she could repeat that feat every three days (without compounding) her annual rate of increase would be 1331 percent. If she could compound her increase at the 11 percent rate, the annual rate would be astronomical. The lesson is to estimate the amount of time required to turn an investment at a profit, for only then can you determine if your estimated return will be adequate.

Equity

Equity is that portion of something that you own. For example, if you purchase a car the down payment is your equity. As you make payments, a portion of each payment is used to retire the principal borrowed, and this—less the amount lost to depreciation—increases your equity.

Equity investments have several distinct advantages over other types of investments. In the first place, you actually own something, a percentage interest in a corporation, a piece of land, an antique, or anything that's tangible. Other kinds of investments, such as options, mortgages, or bonds, do not provide the same kind of security. The difference is, if you own something you may be able to use it while holding it for price appreciation. Even though it may disappoint you and not increase in price, you may still have been able to use it in a beneficial way. And there is still the possibility that it will increase in price one day. Options, by contrast, provide only an opportunity for profit or loss; ownership is not part of that equation. Once the option expires, whatever you paid is lost if you didn't find the conditions favorable for exercising the option. Mortgages and bonds are simply promises to pay. If all goes well, they are fixed-dollar investments that pay you the stated return on your capital. So the best you can do or your investment is known beforehand. The worst is yet to come, as you don't know how your buying power will be protected. Also, such promises to pay sometimes evaporate into default. When that occurs, you have a loss and are left with a piece of paper rather than anything tangible that has real value.

25

In my opinion, the best medium for the investor wishing to build capital is equity ownership. Other investments are better left until you have accumulated your basic capital.

Leverage

Using your own funds for part of the price of an investment and obtaining the remainder from some other source constitutes leverage. For example, you put up 10 percent of the purchase price of a piece of land and agree to pay the balance sometime in the future. The other partner in the venture—who agrees to cover the other 90 percent—normally expects interest on his portion of the funds invested. If your appraisal of the situation is correct and the investment increases in price, the major share of the increase belongs to you. If your buy doubles in price in a year and you sell, you pay off your creditor with 90 percent of the original cost plus interest at, say, 10 percent. The part you keep represents nine times your original investment, or a gross profit (before any expenses) of 900 percent. Your partner in this venture may be a friend, relative, bank, savings and loan company, or even the seller. In all cases they are more concerned with safety of principal and a "safe" return on their capital than they are in capital appreciation. They have their reasons and you have yours.

Leverage is practically the only way the small investor can build capital. All other techniques tend to take more than one lifetime. In some cases, which we will discuss more fully later, it is possible to find a partner in such a scheme who will put up most of the cost at a rate of return that is less than the rate of inflation. In such a situation you are getting the use of his money at no net cost to yourself. It is also possible to "mortgage out" in such deals where the various lenders put up 100 percent of the costs. Meanwhile, you have the equity ownership, and if things work out as you planned, you reap all of the capital gains without risking any of your capital.

Rich

Wealth is more than the quantity of one's income. It also embodies the source of that income. My son asked me the other day if we were rich. He had just purchased an $800 amplifier with his own money, and to him that symbolized wealth. In reality one has to have an *independent* income adequate for one's needs in order to be wealthy. Therefore the widow with $200,000 in income-producing stocks or property is marginally wealthy. Her income is not dependent on a job or salary, and with her home paid for and no long-term debts, her income would exceed her needs. Therefore she would be properly termed wealthy. The individual on a salary is, by contrast, poor, *no matter how high his salary*, for the minute that salary ends, so ends his financial security.

Strong Hands

Application of this concept results in the opposite of leverage. The owner of a property owns 100 percent of the equity. The property is not mortgaged and the owner has no interest in selling. In our society such persons tend to have inherited their capital and along with it a set of beliefs relative to investments. They make good buyers because quality, not price, is their major reason for making purchases. Furthermore, they are rarely forced to sell because they rarely need money. However, one drawback is that they are frequently slow to pay, and they force you to wait while they collect another bond premium. These persons are a predictable quantity that you can incorporate into your investment plans. You can sell them property that you can't afford to continue to hold, while simultaneously owning adjacent or like property. Such action on your part may guarantee an orderly development of your property. If your buyers hold the property and do not sell it, then all similar property that is available for sale, including yours, will increase in value because their purchase results in a reduction of supply.

Weak Hands

Here lies the opportunity for bargains. The owner is forced to sell quickly because his lease expired, he has a payment due at the bank, he is getting a divorce, his company is transferring him to Atlanta, or any other reason necessitating a quick sale.

Settlement of estates is another bargain basement. Often such situations provide you the opportunity to buy below market or even below wholesale. The mistakes of the sellers are frequently of two kinds, a mistake in timing or a lack of adequate financing. The original investment may have sound values which can be realized through waiting a little longer, improving the cash flow, refinancing, or by some other managerial technique. The person selling qualifies as the weak hands; you as the investor can profit by his mistakes in judgment.

Another type within this category is the person who doesn't recognize the real value of what he is selling. In such situations truly fantastic bargains can be picked up, the Rembrandt print that was found in a Chicago garage sale for $10 and resold for $10,000, for example. The way to take advantage of such opportunities is to study that class of investment so well that you recognize the value instantly even under a coat of paint, covered with trash or burdened with restrictions (such as zoning) that you, because of your familiarity, know to be temporary or nonapplicable problems.

Bargain

One definition of a bargain is something you don't need at a price you can't afford to pass up. Great fortunes have been made by investors buying bargains. Normally the best bargains appear when you don't have any money. The spice in the game is figuring out how you can somehow pick them up anyway.

Liquidity

Put simply, liquidity is the relative ease with which you may exchange what you have for cash. For the Penny Capitalist liquidity can become a serious problem. By this I mean too much liquidity is the problem. Standard investment advice is that investments with low liquidity should be avoided because you may need funds quickly at some future date. Therefore investments with high liquidity, those which can easily be converted into cash, are preferable. As a Penny Capitalist you are always in need of ready cash. If your funds are tied up in stocks or are on deposit in a savings account, it is too tempting to draw them out and pay bills or take that long-deserved vacation. What I am proposing here is that investments with low liquidity protect you from yourself and permit your equity to grow.

This technique also protects your investments from the spending tendencies of the rest of the family. Let's face it, if your salary is inadequate, you will always have unpaid bills. The time to invest is now, and the way to do it is to buy a bargain that is not saleable on an everyday basis. For example, in 1967 I visited the local church thrift shop and saw an Indian feather headdress in the sales window. At three dollars it was a bargain, but I really didn't need a headress. I started across the street to leave but then changed my mind and went back and bought the thing. After all, it was old and authentic, and we could get along without the three bucks. Since then we have enjoyed having the headress and have even used it at costume parties. Meanwhile similar specimens have appreciated in value to the point where they are now priced about $600 apiece. My point is that I could have used that three dollars to pay some household bill; I didn't, and somehow the bills got paid anyway. Meanwhile we picked up an investment. To state a Penny Capitalist rule: Low liquidity protects you from spending your invested capital.

Cash Flow

Cash flow is the amount of money you need to pay necessary expenses prior to realizing a profit. If expenses exceed current income then you have a cash flow problem. Certain investments are noted for good cash flow and others for poor cash flow. As a Penny Capitalist, you have a unique cash flow problem: your basic income is inadequate. Stated in another way, in your efforts to make a living you have a negative cash flow. This problem is further compounded by our tax structure. If you increase your income, your taxes increase at a higher rate, so back you go to square one. Building capital under these circumstances becomes exceedingly difficult.

The only way to build capital, then, is through the achievement of capital gains, which are taxed at a much lower rate than ordinary income. However, the best investments for capital gains often pay no income. These are investments with lots of leverage, such as raw land. While your investment is maturing you often have a negative cash flow that is difficult to endure. If, however, you switch to an investment that provides current income, that income is taxed at the regular rate—and your efforts at capital formation take much longer. It is a double box; you can't win either way, or perhaps more accurately, you must forego current income, no matter how difficult that is, in order to build capital for the future.

All of this sounds somewhat unfair to those of us who didn't inherit any capital. My recommended solution—and I hope some of our lawmakers will read this—is that the first $100,000 of earned capital gains per tax-paying unit should be exempt from the capital gains tax. Further, it should be made possible to divert current income tax-free in order to build that $100,000 capital base. Such a plan is similar to Social Security or a Keogh retirement fund, with this important difference: an individual could use his nest egg during his productive life as well as in retirement. The availability of such investable funds would be a fantastic stimulus to the economy in general, and would relieve middle-class Americans from feelings of tax oppression. I propose that such a plan be termed the "Capital Accumulation Allowance."

Bigger Fool

This concept is another way of describing the successful investment. If something was a good buy, the seller was the bigger fool. If it was sold at a profit, then the buyer was the bigger fool. The object of the game, of course, is not to be the bigger fool in any transaction. I'm indebted to one of my friends, The Texas Mall Slinger, for this definition. Since he's made more money than I have, I suspect he has applied this principle more than once.

Other Terms

There are innumerable other terms used by the investment community, *futures, puts, calls, convertible bonds, price-earnings* *ratio*, and lots of others. These refer to specific aspects of investments, and typically they are well defined in the numerous "how-to-invest" books already available.* Since these terms don't apply to Penny Capitalism, there is no need to redefine them here.

---

* A very useful source for the novice is Jerome Tuccille's *Everything the Beginner Needs to Know to Invest Shrewdly* (New Rochelle, N.Y.: Arlington House, 1978).

2

Inflation and Your Investment Program*

Money Is

Even though this chapter is about inflation, I have to define money and how it is used before I can discuss the influences of inflation.

Money is a medium of exchange. You exchange what you produce when you believe that by doing so you will be able to acquire something that you want either today or at some future date. Money permits you to do this through its various attributes. Money may be defined as "a commodity that is accepted in exchange by an individual who intends to trade it for something else" (Browne 1970, p. 16).

Here we get to the basic concept underlying the creation of money; it is *accepted* as a standard of value. In fact, the article accepted as money may or may not have any utility in and of itself. The copper ingots used by the ancient Greeks and the cacao beans used by the ancient Peruvians are examples of money that could have been utilized for their intrinsic characteristics. Other forms of money, such as printed paper or the large, round, flat stones with a central hole used in Yap, are nonutilitarian. They are symbolic forms, with an arbitrarily assigned value that is not linked to their inherent usefulness.

---

* In writing this chapter, my thought processes have been influenced by the writings of Harry Browne, author of *How You Can Profit from the Coming Devaluation* (New Rochelle, N.Y.: Arlington House, 1970). I am most indebted to him.

No matter which kind of money we use, its primary function is to facilitate the exchange of goods. Through the use of money we may prepare for lean times in the future by selling our current excess production and storing the proceeds in the form of money available for future needs. Here the basic monetary concept becomes of prime importance. In order for people to be willing to exchange their current goods for money, they must have assurance that at a future date the money they receive will be accepted at a value commensurate with the value of the goods they exchanged for that money. Therefore, for money to be of utility it must possess a number of attributes, and foremost among these is that it must be universally accepted. In order for that to occur, it must be of uniform size and quality, durable, easily divisible, convenient to transport (the Yap example notwithstanding), and its value must be guaranteed. It is this last characteristic that will take up most of our attention during the rest of this chapter.

You can easily see that most things do not fit our basic monetary requirements for one reason or another. For example if we use pumpkin seeds as our medium of exchange, we could run into problems if they are of different size, or if they have been stored in a pot and nibbled by mice, etc. In such situations assessing the true value of two different pots of seeds poses a problem. Such problems in the normal course of human affairs are settled by agreement, by argument, through recourse to legal action, or by war, depending upon the size and seriousness of the differences of opinion. As a means of reducing these inherent problems, early in the history of modern nations governments assumed the responsibility of creating money. Their action, viewed in a positive light, provides a means to regulate and establish orderly trade through the provision of a universally accepted medium of exchange. In order for their money to be accepted, it had to be marked with the governments' symbols of authority as a guarantee. Initially, those items that were rare, easily divisible, and durable were selected for use as money. In terms of these inherent qualities, the best materials for such use were the metals gold, silver, and bronze. In principle, this system was valid; these metals were rare, they had both utilitarian and decorative uses, they were attractive, and they possessed the other necessary attributes. Unfortunately, when placed in use as coins, pieces of these metals rapidly became subject to vicissitudes that reduced their value. Their edges were clipped or their size otherwise reduced to make their true value less than their stated value. Further, they could be counterfeited through plating or alloying, and the worst offenders on this count were the issuing governments themselves. At least as early as the reign of Nero, debased currency led to the effect described by Gresham's law: the use of bad money drove the good money out of circulation and into hoards.

A solution to this problem was for governments to store the items of real value, i.e., the gold, silver, or whatever, and issue standard receipts (currency) for a fraction of this stored wealth. Use of these receipts included the provision that they could be exchanged easily and at any time for that portion of the stored wealth. This system was in balance when the supply of stored wealth was equal to the total face value of the receipts issued.

Money Does

The next step in the development of money was the formation of credit. Credit is the use of someone else's money in exchange for a fee. Credit is created when the owner of the wealth agrees to lend his wealth for a specified period of time. During this interval he is aware that he can't spend his wealth because he has temporarily given up its use. Meanwhile, the debtor has used the loaned wealth to increase his productivity, so at the end of the specified term he is able to repay what he borrowed plus the fee charged for the use of the funds.

The need for a middleman to handle such transactions led to the development of banks. Banks serve as repositories of wealth and use their depositors' funds in exchange for a fee (interest). The funds they borrow are then loaned to customers at a higher interest fee than that paid to depositors, giving the banks a return for their efforts.

So far everything was still in balance. Money was backed by real stored wealth, and everyone who used this money either gave up the right to use it in exchange for a fee or paid a fee for its use.

At this point, the first flaw in the system cropped up. The banks reasoned, in effect, "If we receive a fee for the funds we lend, then why not issue more receipts for the stored wealth than is actually in storage? The money in circulation all appears the same; how would our creditors ever find out that we have issued more receipts? Only if everyone presented his receipts for the stored wealth at the same time, a highly unlikely possibility, would anyone find out that we had issued too many receipts. Meanwhile, through the use of credit, we will have been earning a fee on much more money than the actual wealth on deposit." The opportunity for gain in this type of situation, from the banks' perspective, greatly exceeded the inherent risk.

At this point in the development of money, governments stepped in and superceded the rights of individual banks to issue money. The opportunity to profit by issuing excess receipts was too lucrative to leave to individual firms. Government sought to control the profits for its own benefit, and the means to do so were enacted into laws that restricted the creation of money. Government became the only issuer of money and the only agency permitted to store wealth.

Then some users became aware that the money in circulation exceeded the stored wealth, and refused to accept the government receipts. When this became a problem, government stepped in again, passing legal-tender laws requiring that government receipts must be accepted if they are offered in payment.

Finally, in order to prevent exchange of the receipts for the true wealth hoarded by the government, and for which the receipts were initially issued, laws were passed making it illegal for the ordinary citizen to own this true wealth and making the receipts irredeemable. Associated with this move was a further step in which government took over regulation of the entire banking system. This sequence of steps placed government in the unique position of being able to create, for its own needs, currency that was not backed by any real weath.

Inflation Is

From government's point of view, the traditional ways of acquiring money through taxation and borrowing have proved to be both limited and burdensome; especially burdensome is repayment! Government circumvents these problems by infla-

No foreign government could counterfeit our currency as successfully as has our own.

tion. It does this in several ways. The first method of inflation is printing more receipts than there is stored wealth. The result is price increases, or to put it another way, a decrease in the value of currency. The second consists of lending to others the funds in checking accounts, which the account owners have not agreed to lend out. A checking account owner has reserved the right to use his funds himself at any time he so chooses. When the government permits the lending of these funds to someone else, two potential users exist for the same funds. When the "real" funds and the "phantom" funds are put to use, the costs of goods and services are bid up in the marketplace.

A third method of inflation is increasing deposits through a fractional-reserve banking system. In the United States the deposits of a bank are used as its legal reserve on deposit at a Federal Reserve bank. At a reserve requirement of 16.5 percent, each $1,000 in deposits may be expanded to $5,000 in loans, or a ratio of reserve to total deposits of about one to six. When the loans are granted they are normally in the form of deposit slips. These "deposits" then add to the sum that supposedly makes up the legal reserve. In fact, as with the other methods of inflation, it is all imaginary money created by writing on pieces of paper, and once again prices of goods and services are driven up.

Supposedly the rate of price inflation can be controlled by

the Federal Reserve System through expansion or contraction of the money supply. In the past, there have been legal limits to inflation, including a limit on the national debt as well as limits on the ratio between the quantity of currency in circulation and the amount of gold on deposit at Fort Knox. The laws regulating the backing of our currency with stored wealth have gradually been removed until today we have nothing left. None of our coins in circulation has had any appreciable real value since 1965, when the last fractional silver coins were minted. The government has redeemed the gold and silver certificates and will no longer "pay to the bearer on demand" any money of real value in exchange for currency. Our government is no longer willing to buy or sell gold in the open domestic market or to establish a ratio between the value of the dollar and the value of gold. The official justification is that gold is no longer necessary in the day-to-day commerce between nations. Gold, in this official view, is a "barbaric relic" that is no longer necessary in the complex and delicate balance of payments between modern nations (no matter that people the world over still consider gold to be a repository of real value, regardless of what governments say). A more cynical view is that this leaves government free to inflate the currency like mad so that it never has to come up with any real wealth to pay its just debts.

There are no real legal limits on inflation. Every time the national debt nears its ceiling Congress passes another law that permits further debt expansion. What few people realize is that in addition to the annual federal budget there are also large numbers of federally guaranteed funding programs. The expansion of these programs is not even subject to the minimal safeguards that apply to our national debt. In short, government has cleared the decks so that inflation can continue to sweep over us unabated. Why is this so?

The explanation for inflationary policies is political expedience. In a normal self-regulating economic system based on supply and demand, as prices rise demand falls, and eventually prices readjust to a lower level, stimulating renewed demand. The joker in the deck is that some potential sellers have established their inventories when prices were high and are forced to sell when prices are low. This aspect of the system is politically unpalatable. No politician seeking election can promise

The antigold forces lose again.

to deliver deflation and expect to be elected, no matter how salutary such a program might be for an overheated economy. The expedient is to increase the money supply through the techniques discussed above. Inflation. The result is an overall rise in prices, and everyone can sell at a profit.

What has actually occurred is a reduction in the buying power of the individual dollar, a hidden cost not apparent to the average individual. Prosperity reigns, and the day of reckoning has been postponed again. Inflation is the hidden worm in the apple. Each pay raise carries with it increases in both the cost of living and taxes, taxes levied at a higher rate. In short, a pay raise is dissipated before it is received. Meanwhile the poor taxpayer, thinking he got a real raise, goes out and buys something expensive on time. How discouraged he is when he finds that after his raise he has less spending money than he did before!

Inflation Does

An example (Fowler, 1973) shows why a $1,000 raise doesn't seem to go anywhere in the face of inflation and a progressive income tax. Figured on after-raise salaries of $13,000 and $20,000 annually, the lucky recipient either has about $15 a month extra to spend as he chooses or ends up in the hole to the tune of $13.33 a month.

	$13,000	$20,000
Additional federal income tax on $1,000	$220	$268
State & city income tax	75	100
Estimated 5% increase in living costs due to inflation applied to all net income for one year, after taxes	524	792
Total deductions from $1,000 raise	$819	$1,160
Take-home money due to raise after considering inflation's impact	+$181	−$160

Now can you understand why your last raise seemed to vanish overnight?

The reason that inflation is permitted to continue is that its source is subtly hidden. Every housewife knows that prices at the local grocery store are increasing, sometimes so rapidly that a single can will have three successive price stickers on it. The housewife blames the grocery store, the canning company, the producer, the trucking firm, and everyone else in the supply chain for these increases. What she doesn't realize is that all of these "villains" are trapped by the system too. Their costs are rising just like hers, and in an attempt to stay in business and make a profit they have been forced to raise their prices. The real culprit is the government, which has caused inflation by creating money that bears no relationship to real wealth.

By increasing the money supply the government has diluted the purchasing power of each individual dollar, and has engaged in a form of hidden taxation. First, any money that the government has borrowed is repaid, both principal and interest, with cheaper dollars. When the inflation rate approaches 5 percent annually, the government is essentially borrowing money free, as the inflation rate cancels out the cost of the interest paid. Further, as a result of the cost-of-living clauses in union contracts, any increase in living costs is reflected in higher wages, and then those higher wages increase future costs, and so on.

Then there is the income tax. How unfair it is to have a cost-of-living wage-increase taxed at a higher tax rate. Think about it. You receive a raise to enable you to maintain your present standard of living, but the increased cost of living plus an increased level of taxation leaves you farther behind. Viewed in this context inflation is a form of double taxation. And you have no choice in the matter, which is why the politicians are so solidly in favor of inflationary programs. Inflation is not under your control, and the government isn't interested in really controlling it.

What does the future hold? I believe the foreseeable future holds continuing inflation, at least as long as the government is able to exercise any control at all over the economy. There will be attempts to limit inflation to a "manageable level." Bear in mind, however, that elimination of inflation is unlikely. Elimination of inflation would require a return to a wage-price structure in which all prices would be adjusted to a standard of production, with wages increased only if production increased. For several reasons, it is unlikely that this will occur. The government would lose its hidden sources of taxation; the large unions would resist the concept of rates of pay being calculated in terms of production; and the individual taxpayer would find his take-home pay reduced. It would not seem as important to the latter that the buying power of the individual dollar had increased. It is the total number of dollars that seems important to him. In short, hardly anyone really wants an end to inflation; most simply want it to continue at a rate that is not so rapid as to cause painful immediate dislocations in the system.

However, there is the constant danger that inflation will get out of hand, soaring at rates of 10 to 100 percent a year. If that happens, the economy will resemble an engine racing at ever-increasing speed. At some point the entire system flies apart. Such runaway inflation is best typified by conditions in Germany after World War I. The currency was continually devalued, and goods and services were priced upward on a daily basis. Eventually it got so bad that prices rose hourly and it cost a million marks to mail a letter! I have a collection of currency from that era. The entire collection is worthless; even today it doesn't have any value to collectors because so much of it was printed. Some bills have been inked over with new values at one-hundredth to one-thousandth their former value. Think about that. What if you have a mattress full of U.S. greenbacks and some day you find that those old bills are declared no longer legal tender since they have been replaced with new bills whose value is much less than the old ones. What can you do with such devalued currency? You can't eat it, or wear it, or do anything else with it that is useful. It has become totally worthless. This is not a vague possibility but a real danger. We will examine this danger in greater detail in the following section.

Inflation and Real Money

Since 1965 our coins have contained no metallic content approximating their stated value. Our currency is no longer backed by gold or any other commodity of value, but only by the government's promise to pay. The federal supply of gold has dwindled, and its price is now determined by the world market. At this writing it is about $170 to $180 an ounce, having fluctuated between $35 and $200 an ounce since the controlled price was removed. Over that time its primary price move has been upward. Since 1971 we have experienced two devaluations of the dollar that have resulted in new relationships with other major world currencies in which the dollar is worth 20 to 40 percent less than it used to be. Silver has increased in value from $1.29 an ounce to $5.00. A Volkswagen has increased in cost from $1,800 to $4,400. The price of oil has quadrupled from three to twelve dollars a barrel. Even with price controls, increased domestic production, conservation, etc., the price of gasoline has more than doubled. During this same seven-year period the total cumulative rate of inflation was "only" 45 percent, according to the figures released by the government.

On the surface it doesn't make sense. If inflation has only increased 45 percent, why do all these other things, gold, oil, silver, foreign cars, etc., cost from 300 to 400 percent more than they did in 1971? The answer, dear friend, is over that brief seven-year period we have had to answer for all those years of inflation since World War II. For years our government had inflated the money supply and simultaneously artificially held down the price of real money—gold—to thirty-five dollars an ounce. When the controlled price was removed, items representing real money were revalued sharply upward. Such an event is likely to repeat itself in the future as inflation continues unabated. You should therefore seek to acquire items of real money (gold and silver) as a protection against increasing inflation. Should the system totally collapse into depression, such items of real money will prove to have been ideal investments. They are the things that will have incredible buying power, especially coins of gold and silver.

I have maintained an investment program in silver jewelry and other silver objects. I buy any silver items that I can find at garage (yard) sales and second-hand stores when they are priced below bullion value. I can estimate weight by hand, and have frequently purchased items at fifty cents to a dollar an ounce. With silver presently at five dollars, I have instant price flexibility. Further, I have a hedge investment for the future.

42

Currency that is no longer legal tender is worthless.

For example, I recently bought a bent silver jar for $4.50. It weighs twelve ounces. At current prices it is worth about sixty dollars. At future prices, who knows? Meanwhile, I can melt it and cast it into a concho belt or a candlestick or some other readily useable or saleable form.

I buy silver because I can recognize it. Silver may or may not be hallmarked and some people can't recognize the real thing even when it is hallmarked. Therefore it can sometimes be purchased cheaply. Silverplate occurs in a form different from objects of sterling and so the two are usually distinguishable. On the other hand, because of its longstanding high value, gold in fabricated form is frequently plated or alloyed. Since I can't easily distinguish real from faked-up gold I don't buy any.

Meanwhile, if real money is increasing in value, what about currency? After all, currency is what we use in our day-to-day transactions as a money substitute. Our currency is assigned a daily value in relation to the other major world currencies. The price adjusts up or down depending on the strength of the dollar as determined by our internal production and our international balance of trade. This adjustment occurs if we import more than we export, with more dollars being sent abroad and held there for future purchases. This decreases the value of the dollar because the dollars held represent a surplus, and any item in surplus is less valuable. If we export more than we import, the dollar is strengthened and foreign nations are in our debt, for we own more of their currencies. Some of this debt is payable in real money—gold—which makes the balance of payments situation so critical. However, this is only part of the picture, for our efforts as an individual nation only partially affect the value of our currency.

The other side of the equation is the management of the economies of major foreign countries. If their rates of inflation are lower than ours, they may be forced to revalue their currencies upward. Consider a young American accountant earning $14,000 a year, and his counterpart in West Germany earning 42,000 marks a year. At three marks to the dollar their earnings are identical. If, however, the German makes a trip to the United States and is able to exchange his marks at two to the dollar because his government has revalued its currency upward, then his effective buying power in the U.S. has increased dramatically. The real cause of the differential is that his government is doing a better job of economic management than ours is.

This situation exists today and it will exist in the future. Any mismanagement of the economy at home is covered up by the overall whitewashing of the entire domestic economy by infla-

44

tion. But when you take your currency and buy an imported car or TV set, or take a trip abroad, the terrible truth comes home. The sins of the government are visited upon *you*.

How bad can it get? In a country where the currency is artificially pegged at an unrealistically high level, a black market in currency will develop. When I was in Egypt the official exchange rate was $2.40 for each Egyptian pound. All tourists were supposed to exchange their funds at the banks at that rate. At the same time you could buy pounds on the street at the rate of one pound for one dollar—a discount of almost 60 percent!

Remember that all fixed investments, bonds, insurance, savings accounts, etc., are repayable in currency rather than real money. As long as inflation continues it is foolish to have much of your capital tied up in such currency-dependent modes of investment. You can protect yourself to some degree by following the fluctuations in the currency market. Currency futures are listed in the *Wall Street Journal, Barron's,* the *Financial Chronicle,* and other publications. Such futures state what current expectations are concerning the future value of major world currencies. For example, at the time of writing, the Mexican peso eighteen months from now is discounted to 80 percent of its present official value relative to the dollar. Surely bad news lies ahead for those Mexicans who are keeping all of their assets in peso accounts.*

It is sometimes possible to buy real money at unbelievably low prices simply because people do not understand the distinction between currency and real money. In 1973 it was still possible to locate silver coins in circulation in Canada. The price of silver at that time was about $1.80 an ounce, so the coins had a bullion value in excess of their face value. Only a few people were aware of this, perhaps no more than one or two percent of the population. Those sharp-eyed persons were rapidly removing the silver from circulation. By 1974 the silver price had leaped to three dollars an ounce, and all the silver coins had been taken out of circulation. The few knowledgeable ones had increased their equity at a bargain price.

---

* This paragraph was written in July 1976. The Mexican peso was dramatically devalued only two months later!

I was amazed to watch this process in action and realize how few people knew what was going on. Yet the same thing happened in the United States between 1965 and 1968. Just think how sweet it was for those individuals who both recognized that coins of real value were available at a discount and had a source such as a vending-machine business or coin-operated laundry!

A Prophet in Time Is Seldom Appreciated

Some years ago, before this book was even a gleam in my eye, I was shopping the annual book sale at a university bookstore. I picked up my first copy of Harry Browne's *How You Can Profit from the Coming Devaluation.* The purchase price was fifty cents a pound! How strange it is that the real prophets are never recognized in advance of the events they foretell! A few months after I bought Browne's book, which was seemingly of little value on the local market, the United States experienced its first monetary devaluation in forty years. You can expect that current and future prophets will be equally unrecognized by the masses in time for their predictions to be of any value to them. Meanwhile, what have those devaluations done for you, or to you? Even if you didn't profit by them, what do they signify for the future? Devaluation is simply a form of repudiation of government indebtedness. The government clears the decks by stating that in the future all of its domestic and foreign debts will be paid off in currency that is worth much less than it used to be. This bails out the government to some degree by reducing its debt load. The dark side of the picture is that it also frees the authorities to instigate more inflation. I believe you can count on continued inflation for the forseeable future. You should plan your investment program accordingly.

In this chapter we have reviewed some of the relationships between real money and currency. We have identified inflation as the real villain in our daily lives and the threat to our long-term investment plans. Inflation can be expected to continue. Knowing this you can plan accordingly. Place your investments in goods of real value. As the prices of those goods grow, ex-

46

change them for currency, but don't hold that currency. Use it to retire indebtedness or invest it in other goods of real value. Divert a portion of your gains into real money (gold and silver) in preparation for the day when the entire house of cards that inflation built comes tumbling down. Be sure that your investments are limited to items of real value—land, income property, antiques, art, gold, silver, etc. Avoid those investments that are currency dependent. Remember that the government plans for you to pick up the tab for its excesses. Whenever that occurs try to be in the position to let George do it, not you.

3

Your Personal Investment

Most of the self-help books on the market imply that augmenting your income is easy. Their authors' rationale is that "anyone can become rich" and that it can be done in a short time if you have self-confidence and utilize their techniques. Depending on the book, it is suggested that it will take from three months to three years to reach your goal. According to these experts, you can start with absolutely zero, borrow your grubstake from a bank or other lending source, invest in something, and presto-zappo you are rich before you know it. They then go on to cite examples of their acquaintances who have done just that. The techniques include rules that you memorize as well as psychological support phrases that in their simplest translation boil down to something analogous to Little Toot saying, "I think I can! I think I can!"

Let's face it, if getting rich or augmenting income were all that simple, everyone would be on easy street. No one would agonize over his budget on the first of the month, trying to stretch an inadequate income over a shoebox full of bills.

What's wrong with the get-rich-quick syndrome? The problem I see in these formulas is that they are not suitable for everyone. The get-rich-quick cases cited typically feature a "go-for-broke" attitude on the part of the investor. He risks everything he has or can borrow on one deal, which if successful makes him look like Superman, when in fact he may only have been lucky. It is even possible that his success was due to the wrong reasons. Bernard Baruch cites an example of this in his book *My Own Story*. He bought and then sold a stock at a

48

profit for a fellow investor. When they compared notes later, Baruch learned that he had bought a *different* stock than his friend had asked for! Often the stories of those who made it big overnight indicate that the individuals involved didn't really know what was going on. In short, they were simply lucky! Those that had bad luck and bombed out don't get mentioned in the success books.

The point I wish to make here is not that such personal success stories are untrue, but simply that they are fairly rare occurrences. You shouldn't count on it happening to you. Tyler Hicks (1970, pp. 194–95) cites a case in which a secretary who didn't know anything about the stock market borrowed $5,000 on a personal loan and invested it in a stock on the strength of a tip from her broker. (She didn't have any financial backing in case the deal soured.) The stock went up, and her broker sold her out eight months later at a $200,000 profit. On the other hand, I can cite the case of a friend of mine who inherited a bundle of stock about 1970. He didn't know anything about the market, and just watched his windfall dwindle during the recent recession. Then, a year ago, he tried to take some action on his own. He borrowed $5,000 and bought Occidental Petroleum stock, which today, a year later, is about where he bought it. During the intervening year it sold lower than his purchase price! So far on that "investment" he has had to make monthly payments and pay 10 percent interest on his loan, has had his capital tied up, and has made no profit. This example serves to make my point that if you don't have anything, and don't know anything about investing, then most of the investment results you might achieve will be due to luck, and a lot of that luck can be bad.

In order to bridge the gap between nothing and plenty you need to make a major personal investment. You need to understand yourself and your goals, and you need to work hard to prepare for that big opportunity. Opportunities to make money are present every day of the week; the question is, Are you prepared to benefit from them? As I write this, I am in a hotel in Tegucigalpa, Honduras. Across the street is a cluster of old one-story buildings covering half a city block. This location is only one block from the central plaza, so it might be a good bet to replace those buildings with a modern ten- to fifteen-story office building or hotel. As an investment it could pay off handsomely. However I will not do anything about it because I am not prepared. I don't have the capital; I don't know the local real estate market; and such a project could well take several years of my time. In short, even though the investment possibilities are there, they are for someone else, not me. This observation brings us to our next topic.

Set Reasonable Investment Goals

We have discussed how rarely really big money is made in go-for-broke deals. Such deals are not for you unless you are prepared to lose your job, your wife, your present financial security, or your health.

How such unfortunate circumstances can come to pass is often ignored by the aggressive neophyte investor. He makes his investment decision, which is followed by a stringent repayment schedule, loan juggling, balloon payments, and other hurdles. Somewhere down the road the investment hasn't quite yet borne fruit, but his wife has had more financial anxiety than she can bear; she wants out. She sues for divorce and it's all over. The costs of the divorce weren't part of our neophyte's investment plan, and they break him. The multiple stresses his investment adventure created begin to get him down, and his production at his job falls off. He gets fired or doesn't get that anticipated promotion, throwing another monkey wrench into the works. Finally, the pressures lead to an ulcer, high blood pressure, a heart attack, or other health ailments. At this point our beleaguered investor realizes—too late—that the go-for-broke philosophy wasn't really for him after all.

Avoiding such a debacle depends primarily on the selection of suitable investment goals. If you wish to maintain a degree of financial and emotional security while initiating an investment program, you should: (1) avoid go-for-broke deals, (2) become informed, (3) realize that you are *not* seeking to become rich, (4) continue your present job as a security blanket, (5) learn investing by practicing small deals first, (6) learn to screen your opportunities carefully, and (7) analyze your personality to determine if you are cautious, self-confident, fool-hardy, self-deceiving, etc.

Self-analysis is the cornerstone of successful investing. Es-

50

tablish goals that are compatible with your personality. In addition, where your goals differ from the personality characteristics of your family you have to take their interests into account as well. A program of small investments will help you with your analysis and at the same time give you practice in investing. Small deals will not endanger your job or financial security. If they don't work out well, you haven't lost everything, but you will have gained valuable experience that will come in handy in the future and help you identify your own shortcomings. Why didn't things work out as well as you planned? Was your analysis inadequate; did events change the direction of the market in midstream; was fraud involved; were you correct in your appraisal but too far in advance of the crowd? All of these things can happen, and if you have had such experience on a small scale, they can be anticipated when you take on bigger deals.

Do Your Homework

Perhaps you should never have gotten into that deal in the first place because it (1) was overpromoted, (2) required talents you don't have, or (3) required greater financial reserves than you have. Remember that most deals aren't for you for these very reasons. Look long and hard for the deal that fits your personality, your talents, your pocketbook, and your time. If you are in doubt about whether a deal is for you, get some help. Ask others for their opinion or to join you to provide talents you do not have or to share the financial risks. These approaches provide a measure of safety because they reduce your overall risk. They may reduce the amount you make on the deal, but during the learning period that's okay. It's better to make a little on a successful deal than to lose a lot on an unsuccessful one. Meanwhile, you have gained valuable experience that you can draw on in the future.

Lots of deals are neither outstandingly successful nor failures; they lie somewhere in between. One of the major reasons for this is broken promises. One of the parties involved in a deal simply doesn't perform according to your prior agreement. Frequently such broken promises lead to lawsuits that involve unanticipated expense and time delays. Since time is money, the effects on your investment are similar. More often, broken promises lead to a reduction in your realized profits, with you absorbing the loss rather than seeking legal recourse. After all, if the loss is low in dollar terms, it may not be worth it to retain a lawyer. On the other hand, remember that any such loss is subtracted directly from your potential profits. Therefore it is to your advantage when initially appraising a deal to pragmatically assess the veracity of any promises made to you. If your judgment is wrong, you can blame anyone you wish, but the loss is yours.

Screening out the potential losers is perhaps more important than isolating winners. At least in the training stage of your career you should concentrate on identifying unfavorable aspects that will make a deal either impossible to close or unprofitable. One of the worst things you can do is invest all you have too soon. If your judgment was bad, you have all your capital tied up and nowhere to go. The alternative is to spend more of your time learning about each investment possibility and categorizing its pros and cons. By this I don't mean that you should become involved in imaginary investing. You should seriously be looking for a place to put your funds, but at the same time be cautious. It has been pointed out that you can invest at will but repent at leisure. Remember, you are just as wrong if your investment fails to make money as if it loses money. Your goal is to make money. Anything less than that does not meet your self-imposed goals. Later on I will point out what the Penny Capitalist's goals should be. At the moment, I am simply pointing out that early in the game your goals should include learning as well as realizing a specific rate of financial return.

Keep Something in Reserve

You may ask, How can I keep something in reserve if I don't have anything? The fact is that you probably have more in reserve than you think. I am including in the concept of reserve your job, your retirement plan, if you have one, your borrowing ability, your life insurance, and your other financial reserves, as well as your time (if nothing else, keep some of your time free; you may need it later to save a sinking investment).

At this point you may rise up in frustration and say, Stop telling me on the one hand, "What have you got to lose, invest now," and on the other, "Keep something in reserve." Hold on. When I refer to keeping something in reserve, I mean that normally you have more ultimate financial assets than you may realize. It is possible to borrow on your home, car, life insurance, and other major assets through a second mortgage or other loan. You can also cash in your retirement plan, borrow from your Uncle Eddie, etc. You can then buy stock on margin, repledge that stock for margin on more stock, or whatever, in hopes of making that big killing. On the other hand, suppose the stock goes down and you receive a margin call. If you are borrowed to the hilt you can't rake up what you need. The result is that you are sold out at a loss, and your entire equity goes down the drain.

When I say, "Keep something in reserve," I mean keep your present financial security, no matter how limited that may be, and begin to build an investment program the Penny Capitalist way to supplement your present income. After you have learned successful techniques of investing, you may feel freer to borrow on your life insurance or use your present wealth in other ways as a steppingstone to future wealth. Keeping something in reserve gives you further financial strength by enabling you to borrow later if a deal hasn't worked out quite like you expected. If the renters move out in the middle of the night owing a month's rent, can you cover the mortgage payment? If not, do you have the credit to borrow what you need to tide you over that rough spot?

Another way to keep something in reserve is to diversify through multiple investments. In that way, if one is not doing so hot, you may be able to keep it going with cash from another investment that is doing well.

One of the major ways to keep something in reserve is to continue your present job. Steady employment is the number one criteria that you need in order to establish credit. With credit you can borrow for investment purposes. Your present job, while paying an inadequate income, may in fact be adequate for your basic needs, such as housing and food. By keeping your present job and building investments on the side you

53

buy the time necessary to build equity without jeopardizing your present standard of living. When your investments have pyramided to the point that they pay you a living wage, you can quit your job. More likely, as your associates recognize your investment abilities, you will be offered a better job, one that more closely fits your newly developed skills.

Make a Commitment

Even if the other guy was lucky on his go-for-broke deal, you may not be, so a more reasonable approach for you is to make a personal commitment that you will invest the time and effort necessary to learn to invest successfully. You can implement this commitment today by beginning an action plan based on study followed by small investments undertaken primarily as learning exercises. Remember that being correct in your investment appraisals and decisions is absolutely essential. You can increase the scale of your investments as your initial successes begin to pay off.

Part of your commitment, then, includes the realization that you are embarking on a long-term course of action that could well take twenty years to show maximum results. Are you willing to invest five years of your spare time to really learn a particular field of investment? If not, perhaps you should try your luck at the race track or the Las Vegas gambling tables. Before you throw this book aside as not for you, however, I can tell you that a lot of investing includes what can be regarded as a treasure hunt. In other words, it is entertainment as well as a means to increase your overall financial health. Later on I'll cite some specific examples that have involved either me or my friends, and some of those have been pretty entertaining.

I believe that a lack of commitment is the reason that so many people fail in their efforts to increase their wealth. They do not investigate fully prior to committing their funds, or they live off the proceeds of successful investments rather than reinvesting, or they bail out of a temporarily depressed situation at a loss because they have lost faith in their own original judgment. Commitment is essential in the search for wealth. You need to invest *yourself* in order to succeed. Success in investing is not a lottery in which you luck out; it is a game you win by training hard, preparing well, and undergoing the sacrifices necessary along the way.

A final bit of advice: don't tell others what you are doing. They will either attempt to discourage you or will fail to believe it possible that you can do what you say. People evaluate everything in terms of their own biases and capabilities. If they lack the courage or foresight to make a commitment, they will find a rationalization for why you can't do it either. But what applies to them may not apply to you. In addition, people refuse to believe that you can do anything until you have already successfully accomplished it. If you tell them you are going to do something before the fact, they will simply fail to believe you. That is why I wrote this book without a publication contract. I have never written a book on investments, and I have no formal credentials in the investment field. Therefore no editor would give me a contract in advance to write such a book. I knew that I could write it, so I simply sat down and wrote it. The fact that you are reading it indicates that my appraisal of my own capabilities was correct. In your own case, do what you know you can do first, and let others find out what you have done when it happens.

Further, many successful investments are the result of someone perceiving a profitable situation in advance of others. If you tell others what you are doing, they may well reduce your profits through their actions! So don't become your own worst enemy; tell only those who need to know about your investment efforts.

As an example of commitment, I can cite the accomplishments of a friend of mine who died recently in a plane crash at thirty-nine. He was a millionaire, he was a U.S. congressman, and he had just won the U.S. Senate primary in his state. He began his commitment as a teenager, when he chose journalism as his college major. At that time he made a commitment to become, when he was ready, a U.S. congressman. He used his talents in journalism to promote a new breed of cattle that he and his father raised. In the process, he developed an outstanding magazine to promote the cattle. The magazine became a success in its own right, growing from a mimeographed newsletter to a full-color publication with 14,000 paid subscribers. When he was ready to run for Congress, he sold his cattle interests in order to remove any possibility of a conflict of interest, converting his existing wealth in cattle to $3.8 million in cash. He was also successful as a U.S. representative for two terms. His philosophy was expressed in his lifestyle: make a total commitment to what you do, and do it well. When promoting his cattle, he said, "When you're shopping for an electric drill, you aren't really buying a drill, you're buying holes." In other words, it's performance that counts, not appearances.

You could well have misunderstood his accomplishments if you read the newspaper accounts after his death, which stressed his youth and wealth. Those of us who know the real story know that he invested over twenty years of hard work, first in preparation and then in performance.

To utilize my friend's accomplishments as a guide in your search for investment success, all you need to know is that your results will be proportionate to the amount of yourself you give to your endeavors.

4

How to Invest

This is the easiest chapter of this book to write, and it deals with the easiest part of the investment process in which to go wrong. Investing in its simplest definition is buying something. Everyone knows that buying is relatively easy. It is selling at a profit that may be difficult or impossible. I have already stated that buying governs the ease with which you may sell. So we should refine our definition to read: Investing requires careful buying in order to acquire maximum real values at the lowest possible cost, a cost below market—at wholesale or even below wholesale.

These considerations change buying from a simple brief impulse to a studied practice based on considerable research. You must ignore the sales pitch of any salesman and investigate for real value. You must be fully knowledgeable about the market so you can immediately evaluate the price asked: Is it too high, average, or a bargain? Only when you determine that true value is being offered at a price below market should you consider buying. Whether you actually buy or not is another matter that will depend on the availability of funds, your willingness to commit yourself to a situation that may require years to prove out, the need to develop a market, or other concerns.

Buying, then, is deceptively easy, because the minute that you buy something, you have tied up your funds. If you bought well, there is no problem, and you should realize your goal of selling at a profit. If you made an average buy then the whole market has to move up before you can recover. If you paid retail, you may not find a buyer at a profit because all potential buyers may be offering bids at wholesale. If you made a bad buy and paid too much, you may never even recover what you paid in the first place, much less earn a return on your investment and recover any associated costs. In the final analysis, buying is the most critical aspect of the investment process. Knowing how to buy is crucial; what you buy is immaterial.

The first act in buying is to research the subject and research the market. If you decide that stocks and bonds—or antiques, or real estate—are for you, get all the books you can find on your chosen subject and read them thoroughly. Read with an eye to identifying the criteria that distinguish things of excellent quality from those not so good. Learn which criteria or attributes affect price changes and how prices have changed over time. Practice your ability by comparing prices asked with your own estimates of true value. Go to stores or read the want ads in the newspaper and practice shop. See if you can identify the items that are the better values. You can never learn it all, so don't be surprised when things sell for more or less than you figure they are worth. Just try to analyze why the price differed from your estimate. At some point, if you work at it, you will realize that the reason the price differed from your appraisal is that you know more about the subject than the buyers or sellers. When you have reached that point, you are ready to buy.

Step One: Buy Something

This step, you say, poses the problem. How can you buy something if you don't have any money? We have already agreed that the reason you are reading this book is that your income is inadequate and you don't have any capital, so it's Catch 22 all over again. My advice—and this is the basic message of this book—is *buy something*. Buy *anything*, as long as it is cheap and you believe it's worth more than you paid for it. This is the Penny Capitalist philosophy in a nutshell. If you don't have any investable capital then begin at the level of investments that cost ten cents to a dollar. Sounds crazy, doesn't it? How can you get anywhere buying things that sell for less than a dollar? Well, the Antique Lady bought a vase for 10 cents and sold it for $65, a mere 64,900 percent profit! A man named Tom

Bolack bought oil leases at 25 cents an acre and sold them for $5,000 an acre. You could do as well. Don't assume that such bargains no longer exist; all you have to do is look for them.

Not long ago I made the following investments at garage sales:

	Cost	Probable Re-sale Value
Pair of Japanese Imari antique porcelain vases	$1.50	$35.00
Silver bracelet, Victorian style	.10	5.00
Egyptian silver bracelet	1.00	7.50
Modern hand-crafted silver bracelet	1.00	5.00
	$3.60	$52.50

My cost was about 7 percent of estimated value. The bullion value of the silver bracelets was about fifteen dollars, or more than four times what I paid for everything. Here is where the principles discussed so far come into practice. Since the bullion value of the bracelets far exceeded my total cost, then my initial investment was doubly protected and very safe. My knowledge of antiques let me know immediately what the vases were and what their approximate value was. At $1.50 they were a steal! With this kind of buying many alternatives are possible. I could sell just one bracelet, or melt it down, and recover more than the total cost of everything, leaving the other items to keep and enjoy, or trade, or sell.

You may note that I have added no costs other than the purchase price to this equation. In fact this is an incorrect procedure, for there were costs in terms of automobile expense and time. However, if you are on the low end of the economy, your time probably isn't worth much, and you can consider the gasoline cost as equivalent to entertainment. After all, if you weren't at garage sales, you might be at a golf course or bowling alley, the movies, or someplace else that costs to visit; it counts as entertainment since it really is a treasure hunt carried out on a small scale.

So, buy something of value. The price is irrelevant, and in

many ways, the cheaper the better. I have bought innumerable items for less than a dollar that were excellent investments. On the other hand, I have never done as well as the Antique Lady with her ten-cent vase. Neither can I remember buying anything of real value for less than ten cents. But one of my friends paid two cents for a northwest coast Indian basket that is now worth twenty or thirty dollars—which goes to prove that he's a better buyer than I am. I will call him the Basket Man because he invested in a collection of over 200 American Indian baskets that later, sold one at a time, put him through college.

In addition to research to identify the good buys, there is another essential aspect of buying. The actual act of exchanging your funds for something alters the entire situation. You are no longer in the position of a student, but have become a practitioner. You have made a commitment. This is the distinguishing characteristic of the professional in any activity. Once you have determined a course of action, you then follow through with confidence and take that action.

The investment world is full of people who diligently plot the daily actions of their chosen stocks. They point to their charts with pride and state that they bought XYZ at 10 and it went to 82, at which point they sold. The only problem is their holdings are all in their head; they haven't actually bought anything. Their reason for doing this, they say, is to acquire knowledge and gain confidence.

This kind of activity is merely training in how to do *imaginary* investing. Real-life investing is different because it's your money out there; every news event can cause your investment either to go through the roof or to plummet like a rock. Do you have the steady nerves to sit there while Libya nationalizes your oil company's holdings there? Or do you panic and sell before you analyze the situation and recognize that only 8 percent of your company's income is from Libya? If your game is only imaginary, you never experience the gut reactions you have when it's your money on the line.

The other reaction that is equally revealing is how long you will let your profits or losses run before you sell. Here again we are dealing in raw emotions. Some people will not sell a loser because that act forces them to admit that they have been wrong. Selling at a profit is an equally frustrating activity. If you sell today, will the price be higher next week?

In a later chapter I will cover selling in greater detail. Here my concern is to impress upon you the fact that the only adequate training for investing is investing. Background reading is essential, but it must be coupled with an actual commitment to a profit-and-loss situation in order to gain experience.

As a training experience to impress my sons with the realities of investing, we bought twenty shares of Telex Corporation. At the time, my boys were eleven and fourteen years old. They made the appraisal of the situation and recommended Telex because they felt Telex had a good chance of winning its then-current litigation against IBM. Two years later we sold, again at their recommendation, and got out with a ten-dollar loss. Telex didn't win its suit, and the stock wallowed at levels below our purchase price for most of the two years. When the general market recovered, Telex moved up to about 40 percent above its two-year low. We sold at a price higher than we paid and still lost money.

The first problem with our Telex deal was that odd lots of stock normally sell for one-eighth of a point less than 100-share round lots. Furthermore, the commission on odd lots is greater. The real-life situation therefore varied from how it would be charted. We made the correct decisions to minimize our losses. We didn't make money for a variety of reasons. We could have bought more shares when it was lower to reduce our average cost, and we could have bought in round lots to reduce our buying and selling costs. All in all, it was a better lesson than it was an investment.

This illustration is excellent documentation of my point; investing is different from talking about investing, reading about it, or making imaginary decisions. The only training for investing that amounts to anything is actually taking a position backed by your own funds. The amount you invest is irrelevant, but the cause-and-effect relationships come into sharp focus when it's your money on the line.

Become Your Own Expert

The next major step in investing is to become your own expert. This procedure is incredibly important, but it is contrary to basic human nature. Everyone has feelings of inadequacy and a lack of confidence. These feelings become intensified when your funds are involved. In fact, a majority of people who are otherwise well-adjusted adults regress to a state resembling that brought on by unreasoning childhood fears when their funds are at stake. Dealing in a state of fear, such people look for an authority figure—the investment counselor—whose advice they solicit. Once they have such advice, they either follow it blindly or follow it partway and then panic at the first adverse news. In either case they have no built-in defense mechanism to preserve the integrity of their capital. They feel defenseless because they don't know anything. They don't know whether or not to trust their counselor. When events prove that the advice they received was wrong, they feel even worse; they feel that they have been cheated. Reality may well be somewhere between that appraisal and the counselor's own opinion of the value of his services.

I have a friend who inherited a substantial family estate. The Inheritor turned the entire management of the estate over to a counselor who, for a 2 percent fee based on the value of the entire estate, managed to reduce the quoted value of the estate by 10 percent in one year. Was the Inheritor justified in claiming foul? The only way to assess that situation is to compare the counselor's track record with that of other managers that same year. As it turned out, that was a bad year in the market, so bad that some mutual funds lost up to 40 percent of their quoted value. In retrospect, then, it is possible that the counselor should be credited with a good performance even though the account lost ground.

The Inheritor felt that there were too many transactions in the account. This is another type of criticism, and relates to the fact that a broker receives a commission on every transaction, buy or sell, regardless of whether that action results in a profit for the client. Every investment counselor has the opportunity to "churn" a client's account, which fattens the broker's commissions and can put the counselor in line for a kickback. Even if there is not an out and out kickback, the counselor can be on the broker's preferred-customer list and be given tips on hot issues that are likely to produce an easy profit. Churning is a gray area that is not watched closely by the Securities and Exchange Commission and, obviously, there can be abuses. Proving that transactions are excessive is very difficult.

The recourse that I recommend is: Become your own expert.

Idiot version of account churning

If you make all the buy-and-sell decisions, then churning will not occur; at least transactions made solely to generate commissions will be eliminated. If you assume the responsibility of making the buy-and-sell decisions, you will gain in confidence and experience. If you leave those decisions to someone else, no matter how competent he is, you will not become more knowledgeable and self-sufficient.

This brings us to another major area of concern: the competence of the average broker or investment counselor. Have you ever called a broker and had him advise you that today is a poor day to buy? Stocks go down as well as up, and figuring on the law of averages, perhaps half the time the proper course of action would be to sell. If you don't have anything to sell, that day you shouldn't do anything. However, this leaves the broker high and dry with no commission. My appraisal of this situation is that normally the broker, or customers' man, is trying to sell you something, and therefore you should examine whatever he recommends with a jaundiced eye. Again we come back to my dictum, Be your own expert. Therein lies safety; any other approach is fraught with danger.

Another major element of this point of view concerns the degree of training and experience that your broker has. There are competent brokers who have a lifetime of experience and who are eminently successful. Can you expect to receive any of their time when all you have is a piddly little account? Chances are, you will end up with the customers' man who has the least amount of experience in the office, probably the greatest amount of overconfidence, and an absolute lack of knowledge of certain market conditions that have occurred in the past but that he was too young to have experienced. The relationship between a broker and client is a delicate one. I don't mean to imply that you should ignore your broker's advice; what I suggest is that you weigh his advice against all other knowledge and experience that you have before you reach a decision on whether to carry out his suggestion. What I am saying is: Don't follow his lead blindly; it isn't his money at risk. In any case, if you follow his advice, he makes a sale and receives a commission. It is a situation in which, heads or tails, he wins— but maybe you lose.

Choosing your broker is as difficult as following his advice once you have him. There's an old saying, "Like shooting fish in a barrel." But you can only hit what's in the barrel at the time. When you call up a brokerage firm as a new customer, you are referred to whomever is on the floor at that moment who isn't already on the phone to another client. In an industry in which the average broker turns over his entire list of clients every four years, a pattern begins to emerge. At a recent cocktail gathering I cornered a local broker and asked how he obtained his clients. He said he (1) inherited them from other brokers who had transferred to another office, (2) was recommended to a prospective client by an existing client, or (3) was on the floor when the phone rang. The system seems to me to be entirely too haphazard when we view what is at stake for both sides. The brokers' attitude seems to be a tolerant one in which they coddle new clients in the hope that over time they will become big clients. Perhaps the answer lies in an organized educational program in which all new clients are invited to seminars where they would not only be taught the essentials of the market but would be given a chance to get to know all of the brokers in the firm. Once they knew the special interests and capabilities of each broker, they could better plan their future contacts with the firm.

If we may return to our basic statistic, that 25 percent of all clients change brokers every year, then we may list a series of hypotheses to explain this turnover:

(1) The client is dissatisfied with his broker and is looking elsewhere because:
  (a) He has lost money.
  (b) He hasn't made enough money.
  (c) He wants another kind of investment advice.
  (d) He is seeking more personal attention.
  (e) He doesn't like his broker on a personal basis.
(2) The client hasn't received adequate services in execution of his orders or in research information.
(3) The client or the broker is moving somewhere else.
(4) The client has received a recommendation from a friend that another broker is better.

It is possible that changing a broker is like seeking greener grass on the other side of the fence. The flaws may exist in the client, but he feels that all he needs to do is change his broker and all will be roses. It seems to me that this area offers a major

65

opportunity for research by brokerage firms. If they can find out why their clients leave so often, perhaps they can institute changes that would alleviate the problems.

Benjamin Graham has examined the relationship between the investor and his counselors in somewhat greater detail. His comments are worth quoting (1973, pp. 131–32).

The investment of money in securities is unique among business operations in that it is almost always based in some degree on advice received from others. The great bulk of investors are amateurs. Naturally they feel that in choosing their securities they can profit by professional guidance. Yet there are peculiarities inherent in the very concept of investment advice.

If the reason people invest is to make money, then in seeking advice they are asking others to tell them how to make money. That idea has some element of naiveté. Businessmen seek professional advice on various elements of their business, but they do not expect to be told how to make a profit. That is their own bailiwick. When they, or nonbusiness people, rely on others to make *investment profits* for them, they are expecting a kind of result for which there is no true counterpart in ordinary business affairs.

If we assume that there are normal or standard *income* results to be obtained from investing money in securities, then the role of the adviser can be more readily established. He will use his superior training and experience to protect his clients against mistakes and to make sure that they obtain the results to which their money is entitled. It is when the investor demands more than an average return on his money, or when his adviser undertakes to do better for him, that the question arises whether more is being asked or promised than is likely to be delivered.

Advice on investments may be obtained from a variety of sources. These include: (1) a relative or friend, presumably knowledgeable in securities; (2) a local (commercial) banker; (3) a financial service or

66

periodical; and (5) an investment counselor. The miscellaneous character of this list suggests that no logical or systematic approach in this matter has crystallized, as yet, in the minds of investors.

Certain common-sense considerations relate to the criterion of normal or standard results mentioned above. Our basic thesis is this: If the investor is to rely chiefly on the advice of others in handling his funds, then either he must limit himself and his advisers strictly to standard, conservative, and even unimaginative forms of investment, or he must have an unusually intimate and favorable knowledge of the person who is going to direct his funds into other channels. But if the ordinary business or professional relationship exists between the investor and his advisors, he can be receptive to *less conventional* suggestions only to the extent that he himself has grown in knowledge and experience and has therefore become competent to pass independent judgment on the recommendations of others. He has then passed from the category of defensive or unenterprising investor into that of aggressive or enterprising investor.

In short, Graham is saying, "Become your own expert." Becoming your own expert has several advantages. Often the best investment opportunities occur under unusual circumstances. Buying at auction is probably the most common opportunity to buy at which you can't count on anyone else to back up your judgment or make the decision for you. Almost everything is sold at auction at one time or another, and it is imperative that you include auctions within your scope of activities because they often provide the best bargains. You can even buy someone's future inheritance at a discount, which, in my opinion, is about as offbeat as you can get. Also, auctions provide the best arena for the self-assured. After all, if something unusual turns up in a farm dispersal, how many in the audience know what it is really worth? Maybe you don't know either, but if you have knowledge and self-assurance, you can take a chance. If you get the chance to buy an Iranian altar cloth for ten dollars, you may not know that its real value is several hundred dollars, but you will recognize that it has a real value greater than the price bid and you will pick it up. What I am suggesting is that you can become both expert at buying and knowledgeable in a particular investment field.

To buy at auction is easy, but it requires following certain basic principles. Some people are afraid to bid, which is the first hurdle to overcome. Don't be afraid, just hold up your hand, and if the auctioneer doesn't nod in your direction, speak up. You can also clarify what the bid is by asking. If you can't understand the bid say, "Is the bid ten dollars?" or whatever you think it is. If the auctioneer says the bid is $110, then at least you know where you are. You can also ask to examine the item being sold, but a better practice is to check everything out before the auction begins and note down what you are willing to pay for each item. Normally you should not bid more than your self-imposed limit on an item because you may be competing with another bidder who doesn't have a realistic price in mind. Furthermore, you may be bidding against the person who consigned the item and he may deliberately run the price up on you.

I attended one auction at which there was a buckskin Indian woman's dress with some beadwork on it. I examined it and determined that the buckskin was commercially tanned, which meant that it wasn't particularly old. The beaded sections extended across leather pieces that had been added to lengthen the sleeves. Therefore the beadwork had been added later and may have been a fraudulent addition by whomever was selling the dress. I decided that if it went for $100 or less I would buy it. When it sold, there were only two bidders above $100, and the bidding went to $900. I am convinced the buyer was bidding against the seller. The buyer was opening an Indian art shop and had the dress priced later at a 100 percent markup. I don't know if he ever sold it, but in terms of real value, it wasn't worth the auction price. It is also possible that my appraisal of the real value was too low, but at least I wasn't the one who paid too much.

Auctions are peculiar places from a psychological point of view. Some are sellers' auctions and some are buyers'. In general, the more people in attendance, the higher the average prices. What is important to recognize is that the bids establish a climate of opinion regarding what things are worth. If the bids start out low, everything tends to sell low, and vice versa.

What is weird is to sit there and watch something sell at what you know is a bargain price and not even bid! I once sat through the selling of uncirculated Mexican silver pesos, eight rolls of twenty each. There were about 300 people in the audience, and those coins sold for six dollars a roll, which at the time was about one-fourth their bullion value. Since then the price of silver has quadrupled, so a $50 investment at that moment would have increased in value to about $800 in four to five years. I sat there like everyone else and didn't even bid. Why, I don't really know, because I knew at the time that the coins were a bargain. However, the prevailing atmosphere at that auction was one of conservatism, and I guess it affected me as well.

There are other places where being your own expert comes in handy. People call you because they know you can appraise the value of things, and they may give you the first opportunity to buy. Garage sales are another setting in which you have to rely on your own judgment. Second-hand stores are also great bargain spots. Again, you cannot rely on the dealer's judgment of value because the best bargains are those that are underpriced. In order to be ahead of the game you have to gamble that your appraisal of the value is correct and the dealer's is wrong.

There are also instances in which a private individual may offer you real estate or something else of value without utilizing a broker, auctioneer, or other intermediary. Such an arrangement can save you the broker's fee, which will usually range from 5 to 20 percent of the sale price. On the other hand, not having a broker involved is not a guarantee that the price is at or below market. The seller may have an unrealistic price in mind, so you have to be your own expert to protect yourself.

In my opinion, no other aspect of investing is more important than that of being your own expert. It gives you peace of mind with respect to the safety of your funds. No battery of consultants can give you the same level of confidence as you can achieve by researching a topic to the point where you can be virtually certain that your appraisal is correct. You know then that, no matter what the current negative opinions are, time and the march of events will eventually prove that your appraisal was on target.

I don't mean that you should ignore all other sources of information; my point is that evaluation of that information is your responsibility. You cannot delegate that responsibility to others without unduly increasing your risk as an investor. This approach also places the responsibility where it correctly should lie. If you have been wrong in your appraisal, then no one else is responsible. You have to accept that fact. If you rely on your broker or mutual-fund salesman, it becomes too easy to put all the blame on him. If, on the other hand, you enter the investment field with a commitment to yourself that every decision is your ultimate responsibility, you will have no one else to blame. To paraphrase President Truman, "The buck stops with you." If mistakes occur, you will know that something in *your* approach was in error. Since it is your own money at stake, you will probably seek to do better next time, or at least to avoid making the same mistake again.

There are two primary mechanisms for becoming your own expert. First, you should read everything you can find on your chosen subject. Especially important are the price lists of items sold at auction. For real estate there are records of transactions. While reading on a subject you should attempt to identify the attributes that signify value. You can then verify your analysis by actual inspection of similar objects or property and then compare your findings against the prices achieved. You have to look very carefully for these evidences of value. Most people do not really examine things beneath their superficial appearance. What actually lies underneath that coat of paint? Are the floor joists eaten by termites, or was the wiring installed before Edison invented the light bulb? Surface indications rarely mirror the true value. For several years I have trained my eyes to perceive evidence of good artistic quality in paintings regardless of their condition. I therefore "see" through the layers of dirt and varnish to the inherent quality of the painting itself, and I buy on the basis of that quality. Usually the price is low because the seller and the average buyer cannot see beyond the dingy surface.

The second aspect of becoming your own expert is to begin buying items of the class you are interested in. I frequently buy things, not because I want them particularly, but to take them apart and see how they are made or how well they may be restored. This kind of experience then prepares me better to appraise other such examples. The only way to cease being a novice buyer is to practice buying; after enough experience you will be able to distinguish value from its imitations.

What You Can Expect

Investments have to be rated in terms of your expected return. The accompanying table illustrates the potential return of investments held for different lengths of time at differing compound interest rates. The long-term return at the higher rates is indeed substantial. On the other hand, returns at the level of current savings-account interest rates minus the rate of inflation and income tax may actually result in a loss of buying power over the term of the investment. Obviously, what is needed is a return that will increase your capital—rather than merely maintain it—and provide some spendable earnings from the use of that capital.

Compound Return on $5,000 Principal Over a 15-Year Term at Selected Interest Rates

Year	5%	10%	15%	20%	25%
1	$ 5,250	$ 5,500	$ 5,750	$ 6,000	$ 6,250
2	5,512	6,050	6,612	7,200	7,812
3	5,788	6,655	7,604	8,640	9,765
4	6,077	7,320	8,744	10,368	12,206
5	6,381	8,052	10,056	12,442	15,257
6	6,700	8,857	11,565	15,930	18,881
7	7,035	9,743	13,299	19,116	23,514
8	7,387	10,717	15,294	23,038	29,392
9	7,756	11,789	17,589	27,646	36,740
10	8,144	12,968	20,227	33,286	46,925
11	8,551	14,265	23,261	39,943	58,656
12	8,979	15,692	26,750	47,931	73,070
13	9,328	17,261	30,763	56,518	91,312
14	9,794	18,989	35,377	67,821	114,152
15	10,284	20,886	49,684	81,385	142,690

If we introduce a somewhat different concept it may help restructure your thinking: What is the power of an investment that *doubles* in value *every year*?

Potential Return of an Investment That Doubles Every Year

Year	Investment
1	$ 1.00
2	2.00
3	4.00
4	8.00
5	16.00
6	32.00
7	64.00
8	128.00
9	256.00
10	512.00
11	1,024.00
12	2,148.00
13	4,096.00
14	8,192.00
15	16,384.00
16	32,768.00
17	65,536.00
18	131,072.00
19	262,144.00
20	524,288.00
21	1,048,576.00

It seems unbelievable, doesn't it? A single dollar invested at an annual rate of increase of 100 percent will result in over $1 million in twenty-one years! Two important points are revealed in this table. First, the initial increase in dollars is slow, so slow that after ten years you are hardly anywhere. Second, the increase in the last four or five years is phenomenal. In my experience you should use this information in two ways.

Invest for Maximum Gain

Obviously you can begin investing with more than one dollar. You should be able to start with a hundred dollars or so without materially affecting your present standard of living. This would tend to shorten the entire process. If you are highly selective in your choices, you may well be able to achieve a 100 percent increase per year for several years. However, as the amount involved increases, it becomes more and more difficult to double your money every year. In addition, after you have built up your capital account to about $30,000 to $50,000, you may become more cautious. The net result of these factors is that you cannot reasonably expect to maintain a safe return at the higher multiples. This means that you must be content with a somewhat smaller return in exchange for greater security of your capital. One result is that the time necessary to reach that million-dollar goal grows. So if you begin investing with $100, at about year eight on our table, and do very well, you may look forward to reaching that million-dollar goal in about twenty years or so. Even if you don't reach it, what have you got to lose if you start now with $100?—only your original investment, $100.

I have not doubled my capital every year, nor have I tried to do so. However, on some investments I have come close. I bought a Navajo blanket in 1966 for $10 and sold it nine years later for $2,000. According to our table, that kind of performance would take eight years, which puts my blanket deal in the same ballpark.

What I wish to emphasize is that if you start out with nothing, you have a right to seek a greater percentile return on your funds. For example, if I had invested my ten dollars in a bond at 8 percent interest, at the end of nine years my capital account, not computing taxes or other losses, would have been twenty dollars. This example serves well to illustrate my conclusion: The difference in return between $20 and $2,000 after nine years is the difference between standard investment practice and the application of the Penny Capitalist philosophy.

An alternative view of the investment potential of your funds is presented by Morton Schulman (1972, p. 10). He cites the actual increase in ICA, a mutual fund, over a thirty-eight-year term. In that example $10,000 invested at a compound annual

Actual Increase in an Investment in ICA Over a 38-Year Term

Number of Years	Period Jan. 1– Dec. 31	If you had invested $10,000 in ICA this many years ago . . .	. . . and taken all income dividends and capital-gain distributions in additional shares . . .		. . . this is what your investment would be worth today
		Initial Investment Cost	Income Dividends Reinvested	Total Investment Cost	Total Value of Shares Dec. 31, 1971
1	1971	$10,000	$ 288	$ 10,288	$ 10,711
2	1970–71	10,000	757	10,757	10,987
3	1969–71	10,000	750	10,750	9,814
4	1968–71	10,000	1,123	11,123	11,483
5	1967–71	10,000	1,701	11,701	14,793
6	1966–71	10,000	1,936	11,936	14,947
7	1965–71	10,000	2,674	12,674	18,961
8	1964–71	10,000	3,332	13,332	22,058
9	1963–71	10,000	4,339	14,339	27,104
10	1962–71	10,000	3,966	13,966	23,508
11	1961–71	10,000	5,112	15,112	28,950
12	1960–71	10,000	5,576	15,576	30,260
13	1959–71	10,000	6,596	16,596	34,557
14	1958–71	10,000	9,855	19,855	50,035
15	1957–71	10,000	8,935	18,935	44,050

16	1956–71	10,000	10,155	20,155	48,786
17	1955–71	10,000	13,039	23,039	61,233
18	1954–71	10,000	20,718	30,718	95,518
19	1953–71	10,000	21,191	31,191	96,027
20	1952–71	10,000	24,090	34,090	107,545
21	1951–71	10,000	28,804	38,804	126,777
22	1950–71	10,000	34,958	44,958	151,884
23	1949–71	10,000	38,617	48,617	165,967
24	1948–71	10,000	39,270	49,270	166,961
25	1947–71	10,000	39,990	49,990	168,365
26	1946–71	10,000	39,335	49,335	164,465
27	1945–71	10,000	54,079	64,079	225,078
28	1944–71	10,000	66,949	76,949	277,263
29	1943–71	10,000	89,211	99,211	367,837
30	1942–71	10,000	104,667	114,667	429,523
31	1941–71	10,000	97,154	107,154	396,744
32	1940–71	10,000	95,286	105,286	387,774
33	1939–71	10,000	96,205	106,205	390,706
34	1938–71	10,000	122,627	132,627	497,666
35	1937–71	10,000	75,828	85,828	306,545
36	1936–71	10,000	107,054	117,054	432,085
37	1935–71	10,000	196,083	206,083	791,426
38	1934–71	10,000	245,727	255,727	991,791

interest rate varying between 10 and 15 percent grew to almost $1 million over the thirty-eight-year period. Again you can see that the greatest increase occurred in the last three years of that period. You can also see the power you can achieve in capital accumulation when you invest at the higher multiples.

Here's another example based on estimated returns. The potential return on $10,000 invested in the stock market in December 1959 is computed according to different investment strategies; returns are as of January 1972, and the figures do not include or take into account dividends, interest payments, commissions, or taxes (Fowler 1973, pp. 304–5). The parable is that several sons were each given $10,000 to invest. Here is how they fared. The figures given are the current values of the original $10,000 investments.

> FIRST SON. Extremely conservative—decided not to take a chance on the stock market and invested his money in high grade corporate bonds which he continued to hold throughout the twelve year period. Very unimaginative. $7,030

> SECOND SON. Also conservative, but he decided that stocks would do better than bonds in the twelve-year period so he put all of his money in the stocks included in the Dow Jones industrial average. But he was both lazy and unimaginative and just stayed with his original purchases for the twelve-year period. $13,100

> THIRD SON. Also invested in the Dow Jones industrial stocks but decided to take advantage of the major bull and bear trends and to be invested only when bull markets were in progress. He bought five times and sold four times during the next twelve years and did the impossible by always catching the major tops for selling and the major bottoms for buying. $51,465

FOURTH SON. Invested only in the five groups that he thought would advance the most in the next twelve years. He too did the impossible and chose the correct ones—soft drinks, up 763 percent, cosmetics, up 517 percent, air conditioning, up 496 percent, coals, up 491 percent and truckers, up 473 percent. $64,810

FIFTH SON. He guessed that there would be fads and fancies during the twelve-year period, so he would try to be in whichever group was most popular. When a favored group peaked out he would shift the proceeds into the next favorite. He was in vending stocks (up 98 percent) from January 1960 to April 1961, in golds (up 30 percent) to June 1962 when most stocks declined, in airlines to June 1966 (up 570 percent), in savings and loans to December 1968 (up 200 percent), in cosmetics to December 1969 (up 30.6 percent) and in mobile homes to December 1971 (up 117 percent). An impossible but excellent record. $1,466,248

SIXTH SON. He invested only in the group that went up the most in each year. $4,749,730

YEAR	GROUP	PERCENTAGE OF GAIN
1960	Canned Foods	48.4
1961	Life Ins.	76.6
1962	Integ. Intl. Oils	13.2
1963	Airlines	99.4
1964	Sulphur	73.8
1965	Radio & TV Mfrs.	132.3
1966	Radio & TV Broad.	26.6

YEAR	GROUP	PERCENTAGE OF GAIN
1967	Bread & Cake Bkrs.	107.8
1968	Savings & Loans	86.0
1969	Cosmetics	30.6
1970	Coals	53.3
1971	Restaurants	103.0

SEVENTH SON. He bought only the stocks listed on the New York Stock Exchange that went up the most each year. $29,750,168,400

YEAR	GROUP	PERCENTAGE OF GAIN
1960	Chock Full O'Nuts	135.6
1961	Korvette	287.0
1962	Natl. Airlines	76.8
1963	Monon Railroad	227.4
1964	Boston & Main	200.0
1965	Fairchild Camera	447.3
1966	Howmet Corp.	139.8
1967	Republic Corp.	1290.0
1968	Duplan Corp.	297.1
1969	Japan Fund	111.1
1970	Overnight Trans.	122.7
1971	Winnebago Ind.	462.3

The examples cited above support the argument that you should follow the advice of Gerald M. Loeb and seek the greatest possible return on your money, for only therein lies the potential for real financial security.

Benjamin Graham (1973, p. 59) has recommended an alternative approach for the small investor. He contends that the young man who saves $1,000 a year should do as follows:

Some of his savings should go automatically into Series E Bonds. The balance is so modest that it seems hardly worthwhile for him to undergo a tough educational and temperamental discipline in order to qualify as an aggressive investor. Thus a simple resort to our standard program for the defensive investor would be at once the easiest and most logical policy.

I couldn't disagree more. I am convinced that the way things are today, the Penny Capitalist has to be aggressive in order to survive. There are too many negative factors at work—inflation, taxation, politics, chicanery in corporate earnings statements, manipulation of prices by insiders, etc. The small investor will forever remain a small and relatively unsuccessful investor if he follows a defensive posture. I believe that a defensive stance is only appropriate for those who already *have* capital.

Perhaps I should further define what I mean by capital. As a working definition, considering present conditions, I see $100,000 of invested capital as the minimum amount one should have before adopting defensive tactics. Otherwise, I regard defensive actions as being inappropriate during a time of continuing "controlled" inflation. Only when runaway inflation (and the inevitable deflation that will follow), is on the horizon should the Penny Capitalist switch to defensive tactics. A defensive posture during continuing moderate inflation can only lead to erosion of your capital. At present, and for the forseeable future, I anticipate only continued inflation under "controlled conditions," which is why I disagree with Graham's advice.

To understand my views fully, you need to consider the basic conditions governing our present economy. It will require a change in federal policies for planned deflation to occur. Our government will have to effect (1) a positive balance of international trade based on a currency backed by something of real value and (2) an end to deficit spending. Only then will inflation be eliminated. So far, there has been little indication that the federal government has any such intentions. In any event, the time to take action is now, and if you start out with only a few dollars, what do you have to lose?

The final step in investing is to keep your account separate from the family budget. What have you gained for the future if your capital has increased by 100 percent over the past year only to be spent to pay a current bill? This is a common problem for all low- and middle-income families. Most likely you can work out some kind of compromise policy under which you declare a dividend, establish an excess-income account, or establish some other mechanism to balance the family's current needs and wants against providing for future needs. What is clear is that if you are to be successful in increasing your capital, you will probably have to include some sacrifice of current wants in order to be able to spare something to invest. In the next chapter we will explore some methods of cutting living costs in order to free up investable funds.

Summarizing the rules set forth in this chapter, you, the Penny Capitalist, should:

• Become an expert on buying.

• Choose and research your investment area(s); become your own expert. Don't buy on the endorsement of someone else; look for real value.

• Set your goals for expected performance, planning to buy only in anticipation of dramatic increases in value and planning to invest for at least a twenty-year term.

• Buy something, no matter how "insignificant" and no matter how insecure you feel about it. Start with inexpensive items and invest for maximum potential increase.

• Invest aggressively.

• Keep your investment account separate from the family budget.

5

Reverse Budgeting

I have mentioned previously the tendency of articles on budgeting to emphasize cutting costs, doing without, and other masochistic methods of living within your present means. And I have asked, Who wants to live on his present income anyway? The problem is, either you have to do without something you need or want or you have to increase your disposable income to avoid such sacrifices. To most people neither of these alternatives seems achievable. But it *can* be done. I will suggest here techniques that have worked for me.

Two considerations seem to me to be most important. The first is how to change your purchasing habits so that you get more for your money. The second concerns how to increase your disposable income. If you can't increase your gross income, is it possible to increase your share of it? Is it unrealistic to seek means to increase your total income? We will explore these alternatives in detail. Our discussion will focus on two aspects, ways to free funds for investment, and ways to increase your standard of living on your current income.

Revising Some Sample Budgets

The *Ladies' Home Journal* (March 1975) published an article on how typical families budget their income, citing these sample budgets:

David Metcalf earns $695.83 a month, plus approximately $45 for directing school plays and speech contests. With $145.51 deducted for income taxes and Social Security, monthly take-home pay is $595.32, budgeted as follows:

Food, household items	130.42
House payment	125.00
Teacher retirement fund	27.83
Union dues	8.80
Electricity	15.00
Heating (natural gas)	10.00
Telephone..................................	7.00
Payment on new refrigerator	20.00
Payment to electrician......................	35.00
Medical bills	25.00
David's education loans....................	123.42
Children's books	6.50
Clothing...................................	10.00
Gasoline...................................	35.00
Car insurance and tune-ups	13.00
Theater	3.35
Total	$595.32

Wayne Meulendyk earns $669.76 a month. With $170.11 deducted for income taxes and Social Security, the Meulendyks' monthly take-home pay is $499.65, which they spend as follows:

Food and house supplies	120.00
House payment	100.00
Credit union (city taxes, major medical expenses, insurance, car payments)	65.00
Master Charge (gasoline, car repairs, druggist bills)	65.00
Education loan	60.00
Heating (natural gas)	30.00
Electricity	12.00
Telephone..................................	10.00
Water	5.00
Clothing...................................	10.00

Entertainment	5.00
Misc. (county taxes, license plates, minor medical bills)..............................	17.65
Total	$499.65

George Schwert earns $626.00 a month. With $125.00 deducted for income taxes and Social Security, the Schwerts' monthly take-home pay is $501. This is how they budget it:

Mortgage on house	130.00
Food	120.00
Utilities, including water, heating oil, electricity, telephone, and cable television	65.00
Bank loan (for George's dentures; Kevin's broken arm)	53.00
Life insurance	14.00
Car, fire, and mortgage insurance	18.00
School and property taxes	15.00
Doctor and dentist bills, mostly for the baby's visits.............................	10.00
Gasoline.....................................	40.00
Store charge (clothes; remodeling items, etc.)	15.00
Misc. (entertainment, etc.)..................	21.00
Total	$501.00

These families living on $500 to $600 a month take-home pay have a really tough time. There is no question in my mind that they are trying hard to make ends meet in the face of what must at times seem to be insurmountable odds. What is most discouraging is that the bulk of their expenditures go for things that have to be considered essential. Where the budgets seem most pinched is in the area of the entertainment and miscellaneous categories, which would seem to provide the only opportunities for impulse-buying and self-gratification. After all, one doesn't exist simply to pay bills! Equally distressing is the limited allocation of funds for investment. The only investment potential lies in the increase in home equity and in one case in

83

a retirement-fund payment. Not included is any calculation of the potential income tax rebate from the standard deduction (now called the "zero bracket amount") plus home mortgage interest.

With these prospects in mind, it seems to me unrealistic for the budget to include payments for any new consumer items. All such items must be purchased second-hand to cut costs. A major reduction in this category would be the elimination of some interest charges (not separately itemized in the *LHJ* examples). The purchase of furniture and other necessary home furnishings could include some items of lasting value, such as antique furniture, rather than throwaways such as Danish modern. The durable items of lasting value would increase in value through time rather than having to be replaced by other cheap substitutes. Shopping the second-hand stores and garage sales for furniture that can be restored and refinished is an excellent first step. Often real antiques with both strength and beauty can be bought more cheaply than their modern flimsy counterparts.

All three example families have the potential for an investment program. All are currently paying on bank loans for educational or other unique expenses. After these are repaid, some funds could be diverted to a monthly investment account. The disadvantage is that such a move would result in a continuation of denial of want-gratification to the point where family members may object and be unwilling to go along with an investment program.

Perhaps a bit more far out would be initiating a tax-exempt retirement fund. However, on budgets this low the most unreasonable expenditure is the $125-plus deducted each month for income taxes. A twenty- or twenty-five-dollar-a-month deduction for a retirement fund prior to the assessment of taxes could result in little or no reduction in take-home pay. The added psychological security might well offset some of the frustrations inherent in a pinched budget.

Cutting Corners: Garage Saling

As I have already pointed out, a major area where cost-cutting is essential is the purchase of consumer goods. Over the years,

I have found that the best source of inexpensive items of every type is Saturday morning garage (yard) sales. Typical items that can be found at these affairs include: clothing, camping gear, sporting goods, bedding, furniture, toys, books, games, magazines, hardware, tools, building materials, car parts, oil, tires, appliances, paint, antiques, lawn supplies, plants, paintings, lawn furniture, rugs and carpets, jewelry, silverware, yard goods, and things too weird to mention.

I have kept some records of my garage-sale purchases. I find that the prices I have paid have averaged about 15 percent of retail. Even items that had never been used and were still in the original packing box were normally priced at 50 to 60 percent of new price. This kind of markdown makes average discount-store prices look pretty high.

By shopping primarily at garage sales the average family should be able to stretch the portion of its budget spent on consumer items by five or six times. Such savings, coupled with the opportunity to find unique items at garage sales, provide a means for self-gratification that is throttled by high prices when shopping in the local department store. A hand-embroidered hostess gown, some ethnic jewelry, a hunting knife, a fishing outfit—these aren't essentials, but they can make life pleasant. When you purchase them at a garage sale you feel you can afford them.

Some families I know shop the garage sales as entertainment. It is the cheapest way of doing something fun. Meanwhile, there is always the possibility that something of investment quality can be picked up at ten cents on the dollar.

Shopping the average garage sale can also be an educational experience. Consider, why is everyone selling these things that show so little use? A primary reason may be that they didn't need them in the first place. Another reason is that items that are rarely used are considered dispensable. If you only ski three times a year, is it realistic to buy new equipment? Garage sales have a kind of equalizing force to them. Once the novelty has worn off a new pair of seventy-dollar skis, perhaps they really are only worth about ten dollars in terms relative to other ways in which you allocate your funds. Far better to pay ten bucks than seventy for something that you value at only ten in the first place.

This aspect of the resale market has been little studied as far as I know. Which items retain more of their new price, which less, and why is this so? What relevance would such studies have for the retail market in consumer goods? I do know that detailed analyses of garbage from urban homes studied by teams at the University of Arizona have revealed surprising things. For example, approximately 10 percent of the food purchased was discarded in perfectly edible form. Another surprise was that lower-income families did not necessarily purchase the most inexpensive items, but rather those most advertised. Further, they did not economize in their purchases of meat and liquor. The conclusion is inescapable: simply because families have little disposable income does not guarantee that they wisely spend what they have.

Another approach to the purchase of consumer items involves a concern for the length of time the item is to be in use. Some items are best rented because the capital outlay is too great for the use benefits. I have rented numerous specialized tools and equipment when needed, including a chain hoist, an electric generator, a pipe threader, and a welder. Other items can be acquired on a shared basis. I have a friend who comes out to cut firewood with his chainsaw. My boys and I provide the deadwood and half the labor; we then split the cut wood fifty-fifty.

Perhaps even more critical are expenditures for items whose use is transitory. The item is purchased, used, and then discarded, all within a short time. My pet peeve is magazines. New magazines cost a dollar or more these days. You can read the average magazine in about thirty minutes, after which it normally is never touched again. It is possible to read them "free" at the local library, and many people do just that. However, the approach I find meets my family's needs is to buy used magazines at garage sales. The lapse in time after publication means little if the magazine deals with a specific subject such as bicycling, photography, cars, travel, sports like hunting or fishing, etc. Even comics seem to lose little of their charm over the years. My boys once bought a whole footlocker full of comics, over 200 of them, for ten dollars. They have been the envy of their friends ever since, and because many old comics sell for high prices on the collectors' market, their trove has investment value too. With the average magazine selling for five to ten cents at garage sales, they are pretty good buys. In some ways, buying a whole year's issues of *Scientific American, Smithsonian, Natural History, National Geographic, Harpers,* or some other good magazine provides an opportunity for better reading than buying them one at a time. When they cost five or ten cents each, it is an even better deal. Now that paperback books cost from $1.25 to $2.95 each, they also are great buys at garage sales, where they normally go for ten to twenty-five cents.

Garage sales can also be a source of the truly unexpected. Some items are fantastic bargains, others are simply fantastic. My brother-in-law bought thousands of new fishing lures and flies from a home manufacturer who went out of business. His cost was about twenty dollars, but his return in pleasure was much greater than that. He also had plenty of lures to give away for Christmas gifts at minimal cost.

The Antique Lady bought a purse at a rummage sale. It had $740 in traveler's checks in it. The embarrassed owner was happy to provide a reward even though the Antique Lady didn't expect one. The Antique Lady also bought a billfold that had a check in it. The check was a promotional item good for a "million laughs" and signed by Fatty Arbuckle. She paid a dime for the billfold and sold the check for five dollars.

The Basket Man bought several dozen handblown and painted Christmas tree ornaments for a dollar. We laughed at him at the time; it was the middle of July, and with the temperature around 100 degrees inside our quonset-hut home, Christmas seemed a long way off. However, he had made a great purchase. The ornaments were genuine works of folk art imported from Germany. This purchase illustrates another buying principle: Buy off-season; that's when prices are lowest.

At garage sales items are frequently priced low simply because the seller can't figure out any earthly use for them. Over the years friends of mine and I have bought some truly unusual items at garage sales. These include a silver ingot, a snowmobile suit, chicken scales, a jeweler's loop, gemstones, a razor hone, a barber chair, a spinning wheel, a hand-grinding wheel, a reducing exerciser, Japanese glass fish floats, abalone shells, gas masks, lapidary equipment, survival gear, and more. Remember, if an item is so unusual that the seller can't figure out a use for it, the price is almost certain to be low. All you have to do is figure out a use for the item and you have an automatic bargain. For example, my family and I have built furniture out of old piano and organ cases. Once such instruments aren't playable, the price is pretty low. Old church pews are another source of good furniture wood. I once bought oak pews at three dollars apiece and built a bookcase. I cut the leftover laminated seats to eighteen-inch lengths, turning them into ideal bread-cutting boards.

Increasing Your Disposable Income

Increasing your disposable income (funds that *you* decide how and where to spend) is a constant challenge. To do this you must reduce your load of such fixed expenses as taxes, interest, housing, etc., by wise shopping, modification of loan terms, and other manipulations. You probably have some flexibility because you have some time payments. Most families have both mortgage payments and time payments on credit cards or other forms of consumer credit. It is possible to shop for credit on terms that meet your needs. The principal variables are the length of time over which payments are to be made, the monthly payment of principal plus interest, the interest rate, and the amount of collateral required, if any.

Whereas it is possible to shop for the cheapest interest rate, that may not be the most important variable. Repayment on terms that are convenient to you is the primary goal. If you can increase your disposable income by fifty dollars a month, which you then invest, the interest differential you pay may be insignificant.

I try to avoid heavy charges on credit cards because the interest rate is 18 percent a year. A good source of less-expensive credit is your local bank. Better yet is a credit union, if you have one where you work. I vary my loans according to my family's needs. We borrow ahead to finance cars, home improvements, and other major expenses. When these loans get paid down to a reasonable level, we refinance. This step reduces our loan payments by combining two or more loans into one. This step extends the length of time we have to pay, but frees up some current income to pay off pressing bills or provides funds for wants or investments.

The main advantages of a credit union are (1) loans granted according to your ability to pay, based on your salary, and (2) the payroll-deduction plan, which eliminates the need for collateral. Thus a credit union is usually the easiest source of credit as well as the cheapest.

My primary advice here is not that any particular credit source is necessarily bad or good, but that your credit needs should be met by means of careful selection. I regard any interest rate above the minimum as excessive, but in some cases it is convenient to use credit cards, even though it costs more. When your credit-card charges with their 18 percent interest get too high, I recommend you take out an installment loan at 10 to 12 percent at your local credit institution to pay them off. This money-saving technique is also good psychologically because it is a forceable reminder that credit-card charges are a part of your overall debt. When you make this conversion, you might as well tear up your credit card. Credit cards are convenient, but they lead to impulse buying. And that's bad. On the other hand, they can be welcome when you spot a bargain and are fresh out of cash. All of this advice boils down to one rule: Manage your consumer credit rather than letting it manage you.

Purchase of a home may be too big a step for many new families. Either it costs too much or you know that you face a job move within a year or two. We solved this problem by buying a house trailer. The trailer was good for three job moves and then formed the basis of our first investment plan. We purchased raw land, drilled a well, built a septic tank, and installed electricity. We then moved the trailer out to the property and began building a house. Costs of rent were avoided once the trailer was paid for, and all we could lose was our initial investment in the trailer itself. Trailer-parking rent was avoided, and those monies could be directly invested in the property we owned. After our new house was liveable, we rented the trailer for a couple of years. Our bookkeeping looked something like this:

Costs		Benefits	
Trailer	$2,400	7 years' rent avoidance @ $100 per mo.	$8,400
Lot rental	1,500		
Land	1,250	Trailer rent received	960
Well	2,000	Total	$9,360
Electricity	125		
Septic tank	150		
Total	$7,425		

The costs included interest on our payments as well as taxes, but in any event, I believe you can see how the rent saved enabled us to invest in a permanent piece of property. The only nonrecoverable costs were depreciation on the house trailer plus interest, totaling about $2,700, plus the lot rental of $1,500. The total benefit of income and avoided rent payments of $9,360 less these nonrecoverable expenses netted us $5,160 to invest in our future home. At the same time we had a low average monthly housing cost.

The purchase of a home is a big step resulting in the largest single payment to be made out of take-home pay. Wise shopping is critical here. When shopping for our present property we compared two packages in the same area. The one we bought had more land, a better house, and a barn, all at lower monthly payments than the other property. The difference was in the financing. Financing is crucial. In this case we assumed an existing mortgage at 6 percent interest. The previous owners had paid on the mortgage for five years, with their total payments as follows: interest $7,162.26, principal $4,090.82. In the month that we assumed payments the principal portion of the monthly payment for the first time exceeded the interest portion. This kind of deal is better for the buyer than the seller.

The net result is that a buyer who assumes an existing mortgage builds equity faster for the same out-of-pocket monthly cost as the seller had to handle because a higher precentage of the payment is applied to paying off the principal. The house we didn't buy cost less, but had a mortgage on a shorter term, fifteen years instead of twenty-five. The difference meant a higher monthly payment on the cheaper property, which, while paying off the loan faster, would have left us strapped to make the necessary improvements on the lower-quality house. The more expensive property was the better bargain because we got more in assets at a lower monthly cost. The march of inflation since that purchase has doubled the market value of the property. Since my salary has only increased 64 percent in the same interval, it is obvious that we couldn't afford to buy the same property today.

Shopping for housing is truly a fascinating experience. You need so many rooms, so much land, accessibility to shopping and schools, and so on. Houses meeting these requirements come in different packages, both in terms of assets and in the financing. Careful shopping will maximize your investment potential and protect you against hidden problems such as termites, old plumbing, inadequate wiring, an assessment for paving, etc. No property will be without problems but you should investigate carefully so that there won't be any unpleasant surprises after you move in.

Perhaps the most important caveat is: Don't trust your real estate agent. Real estate agents are the most slipshod, inadequately prepared "professionals" I have ever dealt with. They routinely are uninformed about vital aspects of the properties they have listed. As a result, you can expect to be surprised later if you don't act as your own expert in the shopping process. In our case, one agent made a mistake in a sales contract that upped the price to $1,000 above the price we were offering. He also failed to tell us about a legal restriction on the property that limited subdivision rights. Our lawyer had to find that one out for us. Another agent told us a rental property was rented at seventy dollars a month. When we checked with the renters, we found they were paying half that! Another caveat: If you want any repairs made by the sellers, get it in the sales contract. The sales agent will try to avoid this because it may kill the sale. But remember, after the sales agreement is signed it is too late. Be firm, don't trust any real estate agent, and be prepared to lose out on a property occasionally. If you know what you want and stick to it, you will usually get it—and you might even get a better deal.

Finally, in your analysis of whether to buy a home or not, do not overlook two potential areas of savings and profit. The interest and property taxes are deductible for income-tax purposes, which usually results in a lump-sum refund once a year. This fact should be included into your calculations of how large a mortgage payment you can afford. The second potential profit-savings factor is the increase in the value of your equity in your house resulting from inflation. If you don't buy, the buying power of your nest egg may decline if placed in an alternate investment.

Why Not Moonlight?

If you can't make ends meet by cutting costs and increasing your disposable income internally, then your only recourse is to increase your gross income. In my opinion it is best to identify what you want and seek means to achieve it rather than to cut back your wants to fit your budget. After all, there's certainly nothing wrong with a commitment to work overtime or on a second job if it provides the extra income you need to achieve the standard of living you want. I know a concert violinist who sells cider beside the highway on weekends, and a professor of English who sells oriental rugs on the side. Lots of avenues exist for extra income. Major corporations such as Avon and the Fuller Brush Company depend on part-time salesmen. One of my friends, whom I will call the Fastest Trader in the West, prefers buying something at a bargain price and reselling it later because that technique takes less of his time relative to the increase in his income or price flexibility.

One advantage of the part-time income is that it is more easily identified as extra. It can therefore be more easily justified as income suitable for investment than can funds squirrelled away out of the family budget. The latter practice can only lead to feelings of frustration on the part of family members whose priorities may not include investing for the future.

Think of the advantages if your part-time earnings are in a field in which investing opportunities are part of the daily routine of doing business. A part-time real estate salesman or broker-age assistant has opportunities that never are presented to the supermarket checker.

The primary problem to avoid with your extra earnings is buying a new car or some other major consumer item simply because you now have the income to make the payments. Put that extra income into some kind of income-producing or cap-ital-gain-producing investment. Only in that way will you be able to work less and enjoy life more in future years.

Something for Nothing

Finally, what can you get for nothing? The best opportunities for free items are associated with building materials. When old buildings are torn down you can frequently pick up bricks, lumber, windows, and such simply for hauling them away. The local junkyard may also serve as a source of free useable ma-terials. Often contractors putting up new buildings are glad to have the waste materials hauled away. Their carpenters are so highly paid that they can't afford to let them use short pieces of wood or odd-shaped pieces of paneling. If your time isn't so valuable, you can probably put those items to good use. You would be surprised what some people consider throw-aways. Once we were *given* a nine-by-twelve oriental rug because the owner no longer had need for it!

People conducting garage sales are often moving, and you may be able to make a deal with them for things that they would otherwise have to spend time hauling to the dump. In one such case, I was given an old carpenter's chest after it had been abandoned in a shed and suffered water damage. I refin-ished the chest and replaced the warped boards. It is made of pine and walnut and has the original brass hardware. Restored it is worth several hundred dollars. I once made a coffee table out of a piano that had been ruined by a flooding bathroom.

Another example of turning waste materials into valuable equities is the time a friend and I scoured the town after a really bad windstorm, asking homeowners for permission to remove trees that had blown down. We came up with three walnut trees and a maple. Sawed into lumber they are quite valuable. We have sold some to home-furniture makers, traded some to sculptors and gunsmiths, and still have a twenty-year supply on hand. Our cost was approximately $100 for the sawing. We even removed the stumps. (The easiest way to do this is to dig around the stump and chop the roots. When you have it reasonably exposed call an automobile wrecker. He can hook onto the stump with his winch and boom and pull it just like a dentist pulls a tooth.)

One day the Basket Man and I visited the local dump. While we were there some people came up and dumped a single-size brass bed. The Basket Man said, "Don't you want that?" They replied, "If you want it we have another just like it at home that you can have too"! That pair of antique brass beds is worth about $500 on today's market, and my friend's cost was zero.

While my family and I were building our house in New Mexico, we were given the salvage rights to an abandoned adobe house for fifty dollars. We salvaged 4,000 adobe bricks worth about thirty cents apiece and roof beams sufficient for two rooms. We also obtained free logs for other roof beams, courtesy of the U.S. Forest Service. They had improved a forest road and trees cut alongside the road were free for the handling.

These examples show that just because items are free doesn't mean they aren't valuable. Getting things free is one of the best possible ways to increase your equity that I know.

Here's another example. A friend of mine was given an entire set of government publications by his hometown library. He kept those he wanted and asked if I wanted those on geology, which I did. There were 207 clothbound and numerous paperbound volumes, all published by the U.S. Geological Survey. Most were published between 1907 and 1913. For years I tried to sell them to a library without success. Secondhand book dealers wouldn't even answer my letters of inquiry. After about fifteen years I finally sold them to a geologist for $250. I immediately reinvested the proceeds in an English grandfather clock made around 1790. Today the clock is worth between $750 and $1,000. My original cost was twenty dollars in shipping charges on the books.

This brings us to another rule for building equity. Just because there are no buyers doesn't mean that what you have is worthless; you may have to wait for a buying interest to develop. For example, most of you can remember when old comic books were worthless. Today they have auctions where they sell at high prices and conventions where they are sold and traded.

To sum up the basic rules of reverse budgeting:

- Cut your consumer costs by buying at garage sales.

- Buy worthwhile antique furniture and refinish it. It is a better buy for the money and will increase in value rather than depreciate as modern furniture does.

- Shop for the better bargain in housing, especially look for the better deal in the financing package.

- Consider a house trailer as an initial method of simultaneously cutting housing costs plus building equity.

- Investigate the establishment of a retirement fund as a means of reducing your income tax load.

- Refinance to increase your disposable income. Manage your credit rather than letting it manage you.

- Don't ignore the possibilities for increasing your income through part-time activities.

- Be alert for things you can get free.

6

Nothing Ventured, Something Gained

Investing on a Shoestring

The standard concept of investing assumes that you have an equity in cash as a start. This equity is invested in something in an equation that varies from partial ownership to total ownership. You exchange your cash for ownership, which ranges from an accepted low of 10 to 20 percent in real estate to as much as 100 percent of the purchase price in the case of most individual items or shares of stock. The difference between your equity ownership and the full purchase price is acquired by a loan and is called *margin*.

The provider of the loan normally expects to hold a lien or mortgage on the property until you have repaid the loan. Standard practice in lending assumes that you have a cash equity in the property. This provides extra safety for the lender. His view is that, if the property decreases in value and you are forced to sell, the market value may still approximate his outlay.

This practice is biased totally in favor of lenders. They do not necessarily wish you ill, but they do wish to have their interests protected to the full extent of the law. The initial risk is thus lumped onto you, the poor investor, who put up your own hard-earned cash. Only if there is a major market bust do the lenders assume any risk. For example, if you put up 20 percent of the purchase price of something, borrow 80 percent from a bank, and later sell out at a 25 percent loss, you lose 100 percent of your invested capital and the bank loses only 6 percent of its capital. For assuming this kind of risk the bank charges you interest of 9 to 10 percent a year. It is a better deal for the mortgage holder than it is for the investor, especially when the down payment required is often more like 25 to 30 percent of the purchase price.

How to Mortgage Out

There is a technique that can work to your advantage in such situations. It is called mortgaging out, and it can reduce your risk. The technique consists of arranging for two simultaneous mortgages on the same property. Your cash input at the beginning of this arrangement is zero. However, if you have made a good purchase, at a price below market, you may in fact have achieved an equity simply by signing the purchase contract. Realtors call this "sweat equity," and it can also be arranged by getting several partners to invest in the property. For example, four partners each pay 25 percent of the cost but each receives 20 percent ownership. You, as the project manager, retain 20 percent of the equity for your participation in putting the deal together.

Another arrangement is to get a first mortgage from a standard lending agency and get the seller to agree to carry the balance on a second mortgage. We did this on forty acres we bought in 1971. The seller carried 50 percent on a ten-year payout and we arranged with a mortgage company for a thirty-year loan on the balance, with no principal payment due for two years. Our initial costs didn't even include a realtor's commission because we dealt directly with the seller. Our costs included lawyers' fees and deed transfer fees. In the seven years since then the market value of the property has tripled. We now have an equity worth more than the total 1971 selling price. Meanwhile, we have enjoyed income from sales of hay and rent of pasture plus an income tax rebate on interest paid. Our total annual out-of-pocket costs have averaged between $1,000 and $2,000. Our net increase on invested capital is in the vicinity of 1,000 percent. When the seller and I first discussed the deal I had five cents in my pocket!

The standard practices concerning buying on margin and

using leverage are established for the benefit of the lending institutions. They want both the *highest* possible return on their equity and the *lowest* possible risk. Doesn't sound quite fair to you, does it, especially when you consider that they are depending on you in order to stay in business?

There are ways to beat the system. A friend of mine, whom I call the Apartment Pyramider, borrowed the maximum on each of his three credit cards. He used this as a down payment on a low-priced rental house. He then raised the rent and went back to the bank with this evidence of the increased earning power of the property and refinanced. He then took funds from the new mortgage and paid off the credit loans. At this point his cost for the equity was zero. He then sold the house for enough to provide a down payment on a rundown ten-unit apartment house. He raised the rent, refinanced, and repeated the process. Today, some six years later, he has an investment equity of several hundred thousand dollars and is shopping for million-dollar apartment units and business buildings.

The key to such a pyramiding operation is an "up" market. Inflation is your strongest ally. Another major factor is that lending institutions are inherently conservative. They lend funds on a conservative appraisal of today's conditions. They will not or cannot believe that a property will return more income in the future. You must first raise the rent and then the bank will agree that such a possibility is indeed feasible. As long as inflation continues, such opportunities to increase equity will be commonplace. When you invest in this fashion, your overall percentile increases in equity can be fantastic. The attitude of the mortgage institutions is, If you have no cash invested, you have nothing to lose. They are wrong; you have everything to lose—your chance to build capital in a "managed" economy in which income taxation penalizes the building of capital.

Another basic tenet of getting something for nothing concerns dealing in multiples. If you buy one acre or one rental unit you become the ultimate consumer and pay the associated retail price. If you buy forty acres or a twenty-unit apartment house your costs per acre or per unit are greatly reduced. In addition to the advantages of lower unit costs, the percentage of equity required is frequently less. Economies are thus realized that will again be reflected in your return on equity invested.

A good example concerns the price per acre of raw land in the county in which I live. Prices of one- to two-acre properties range from $5,000 to $10,000. Average prices on properties in acreages of 40 to 100 acres are in the $1,000- to $3,000-per-acre price range. How this multiple can work to your advantage is well illustrated by the following example.

We had a teacher friend who had $10,000 to invest in raw land. She wanted to pay cash and not have any mortgage to pay. We shopped all the listings and could not buy for cash any tract larger than two acres for the $10,000 available. As an alternative, another friend and I formed a partnership with her and bought 100 acres with a down payment of $10,000. The price was only $30,000, so we assumed a mortgage of $20,000 provided by the sellers. Our teacher friend owns a third, and the other partner owns a third. The entry cost to the other partner and me was zero, but we assumed the mortgage payments of $158 a month. The property has an old cabin on it, which we remodeled for $5,000. The cabin now rents for $150 a month. After three years the rent has equaled our initial investment in remodeling costs and is paying off the mortgage. However, we recovered our remodeling costs in another way. We sold an undivided 10 percent interest in the property for $5,000 and paid off the bank loan for the remodeling. Therefore, at this time we own 23 percent of the land plus one-third interest in the remodeled cabin. The rent carries the mortgage and we have a free ride. Our total investment costs so far are minimal. The deal was excellent for us, but it was also good for our friend because she acquired thirty-three acres free and clear for her $10,000 cash. We also followed our first rule of investing by buying property at a price below the average market. Furthermore, the property has additional potential values in gold, silver, and lead mineralization. It was mined prior to 1910 and may again be worth mining someday. Our cost for the mineral potential was zero, as the price per acre was based on land values established for housing.

Another something-for-nothing deal was when we entered the purebred cattle business. We borrowed the $1,500 down payment on the cattle from our credit union. We had the land so the feed was already provided. The seller of the cattle provided the credit for the remainder of the purchase price of the animals on a two-year term. We bought three cows with three calves. During the two years of indebtedness, the cow herd could be expected to double in size, and we would have some calves to sell. The plan worked reasonably well, and five years later our herd had grown to about thirty head. We have had to add funds from other sources in order to meet the carrying costs of the herd because the animals usually aren't sold until they are two years old. However, the principle remains the same: we made an investment using none of our own funds, and there has been a rapid increase in equity over time.

Another way to get something for nothing is to buy two items at bargain prices and then sell one for the total cost of both. The item kept may well be the more desirable of the two, and its ultimate cost to you is zero. This system works if you sell one item relatively quickly. If not, you should in fact charge a cost to your investment equivalent to the sum of potential interest lost.

As I showed in the last chapter, just because something has been thrown away, it doesn't mean it is worthless. The act of discarding by someone else doesn't alter the item's value; the discarder may simply not have recognized the real value. For example, when I was a teenager I found a silverplated tea service in a local dump. We had it resilvered, and now, after some thirty years, it is a family heirloom. My father-in-law found several thousand shares of Alaska International Corporation at the city dump. They are probably worthless. However corporate affairs are involved, and it is always possible that in the future those shares may be worth something. Meanwhile it costs nothing to keep them.

The Power of Cash

In an expanding inflationary economy no one has any ready cash. Everyone is borrowed to the limit. This situation is ready-made for the small investor with limited capital. Margin requirements are relaxed and down payments are low. Meanwhile, some owners have become overextended and for tax reasons or the need for liquidity have decided to sell. In an overheated economy they can't find buyers with money. Frequently they will transfer title to you for a ridiculously low cash down payment simply to get out from under their repayment schedule.

One such situation involved friends of ours who bought a $50,000 house for a $2,400 down payment and closing costs. The $500 monthly mortgage payment was too great a burden for the seller to continue. He offered the buyers assumption of the existing first mortgage and carried the balance on a second mortgage himself for two years, with interest-only payments. The buyers had a balloon payment of $9,000 due at the end of the two years. By the time this came due, however, their equity had increased more than that as a result of inflation. Then they had the option of refinancing the entire balance, paying off the second mortgage, or refinancing the second mortgage. In any event, their equity risk was minimal, and the original cash investment amounted to less than 5 percent of the purchase price.

The Apartment Pyramider bought the thirty-unit apartment house I mentioned in the preface. When I considered buying it, I asked the realtor about the terms. I was told that the $400,000 unit would require a $50,000 down payment. The deal was eventually closed with a $30,000 down payment, with a balance of $20,000 outstanding, besides the mortgages, due in two years. This gave my friend two years to find a buyer, refinance, or pay off that $20,000 out of increased rents. As it turned out, he needed more time, but the principle of buying with a low down payment is still valid.

On the other hand, in an expanding economy in which cash is at a premium, a 100 percent cash offer can often lead to a substantial reduction in a purchase price, often up to 20 percent. After all, if you as the seller can reinvest the sale price with great leverage, such a discount is reasonable. We sold our first house that way. The buyers offered a lower price than we were asking, but it was 100 percent cash. Another interested party wanted us to carry the mortgage on a twenty-year payout. The difference was impressive. We took the cash offer and immediately reinvested in our present property. By using the entire equity in our first house as a down payment for the second, we achieved a quantum jump in house quality. Another variant of this method is to shop with cash, buy at a discount, and immediately refinance and get your original investment back while retaining an equity position in your purchase. Even if you mortgage out and have mortgages outstanding to an amount equivalent to 100 percent of the current assessed valuation of the property, you are still the legal owner. If the property increases in value, all of this increase accrues to you.

Something for nothing also includes the unexpected qualities of equity ownership. Serendipity if you wish. I've mentioned the gold, silver, and lead on our mountain land. Another bonus on our farm property was the water rights sold with the land. These water rights are shares in the local irrigation company. They are issued as shares of stock independent of the title to the land itself. This means that these shares are separate property. They are not mortgaged with the property, but may be used separately as collateral for a loan or be sold. In a sense they were free sources of equity because they did not add to our indebtedness and can be itemized as an equity asset.

A perhaps more spectacular example of serendipity is that of one of my friends who owns property with several old mines. In one of the mines he found some jars of sand with a large increment of gold dust. Not a bad hidden asset!

While I am discussing something for nothing, I can't leave out the great Jim Beam whiskey-bottle boondoggle. It was short lived, but enjoyable while it lasted. The bottles were decorative decanters filled with Beam's best whiskey. During the 1960s there was a flurry of activity in the collecting of these commemorative bottles. We bought the bottles in liquor stores for ten to twelve dollars each, drank the contents, and resold the bottles for more than we paid for them! The teetotalers in on the deal went a step further. They bought the bottles and poured the contents down the drain before reselling. This impossible situation continued for several years before the supply exceeded the demand and the bottle market collapsed. But it was great while it lasted!

Other items that can be obtained at no cost may have no particular market value, but by their uniqueness may serve a function. For example, one of our sons was given a prop left over from the high school stage play, built of plywood and gold

102

painted cloth. The six-foot-plus prop would serve as an addition to any teenage boy's room. Perhaps not everyone would want a replica of King Tutankhamen's gold sarcophagus in his room, but my son is the envy of his friends.

To recap, these are the basic rules for acquiring something for nothing:

- When in doubt, mortgage out.

- Mortgage out any other time you can.

- If someone offers you something free, take it. You can always discard it later if you can't find a use for it.

- Look for discarded or unwanted items.

- Look for hidden assets when buying property.

- When buying property don't overlook the power of cash. Even a small amount of cash may be sufficient to make the deal possible.

- Find partners to put up the cash and earn your share of the equity by managing the project.

7

Credit Roulette in Action

Borrowing money is neither a stigma nor a panacea. The Penny Capitalist should view the use of credit as a necessary step in the acquisition of the capital he needs.

Unfortunately, the rules of borrowing are difficult to fathom. In my opinion, the principal lending agencies, banks and savings and loan companies, are remarkably secretive and perverse in their dealings with their customers. The average customer is faced with a system in which, when he signs the bottom line of the loan agreement, he signs underneath the term *Debtor*, hardly an atmosphere which leads to friendly relations between a business firm and its customers. In some ways I don't understand how these credit institutions do any business at all. They don't advertise their interest rates or their terms, and the investor seeking capital has to invest an enormous amount of time going from one bank to another talking to loan officers in order to get the picture. Each bank likes to think that they can provide all your needs, but at the same time in their loan officers' meetings they agree that certain kinds of property will not be accepted as collateral or that they will only provide loans on terms that are unacceptable to some responsible borrowers.

We have a real estate loan on our house with a local bank. When we wanted to purchase the adjacent forty acres, our bank offered to lend 50 percent of the appraised value on a five-year term at 8 percent interest. We eventually got a loan from an agricultural lender who offered 50 percent of the appraised value on a thirty-year term at 7.5 percent interest, with only

Key your loan needs to the interests of the lender.

interest due for the first two years. The difference in the monthly payment was staggering. Our "full service bank" had a policy to support loans on urban property, and raw land simply was not anything they understood or would support. They don't know anything about the cattle business either, so we had to find an agriculturally oriented bank to help out there.

Meanwhile, the average borrower is trying to locate a source of funds for his particular investment. What he doesn't realize is that his credit rating may be fine, but the bank has refused his loan for reasons that pertain to bank policy. So rule one of borrowing money is to locate a credit source that routinely loans money on the type of purchase that you have in mind.

The next step in acquiring funds is filling out a credit application. The credit application is usually a short form itemizing your assets and current outstanding liabilities. The latter serve as sources for the credit officer to check to determine if you pay your bills promptly and whether you have defaulted on a note at any time in the past. If you are clean, the process can still get sticky if some deadbeat with the same name as yours has been running up bills all over town. Computers can also louse up your credit rating by billing you for charges you never made.

Most people wait until they have selected a car or a house to establish their credit for the purchase. A better system is to see the loan officer first. Fill out the credit application and begin looking for that car or house the next week. This arrangement gives you additional buying power because the banker will have approved your credit in advance. When buying, you then can write a check for the entire amount, or at least the earnest-money payment to accompany the sales contract. This technique gives you the further advantage of being able to bargain with cash in hand. The cost savings can range up to 20 percent, which goes a long way toward meeting your interest charges.

We should at this point distinguish between different types of credit. In general, there are three categories: consumer-credit installment loans, credit cards, and charge accounts; real estate mortgages; and lines of credit established for business purposes. Most people deal only in the first two categories and plan to repay the amount borrowed out of their future salary. With such loans, credit managers have a rule of thumb that the

106

average borrower can borrow no more than one-third of his annual income, not counting the sum borrowed on his home mortgage. Additional sources of income, such as those provided by a working wife or nonsalaried activities such as freelance efforts on weekends, are heavily discounted. However, this rule can be circumvented easily by the determined borrower who borrows to the limit on a bank installment loan first and then borrows to the limit on his various credit cards. If these proceeds are used for intelligent investments, it may be a wise course of action. To do the same to finance a vacation or the purchase of more new consumer goods is financial suicide.

When in Doubt, Call It Collateral

One way to increase your borrowing power is to acquire collateral. With collateral pledged, a lending agency will be somewhat more liberal in the amount loaned because it has a legal right to the property pledged in case you default.

A definition of collateral is difficult to provide. In general, it consists of any item a lender is willing to accept as a guarantee on a loan. In practice, however, most collateral accepted is limited to things that are transferred by title—stock, automobiles, real property, etc. The reason for this is that the bank has no real mechanism for repossessing such things as your piano or TV set. From its point of view such collateral is a nuisance; it is bulky, difficult to dispose of, and can't be retained on file until the loan is paid. For loan purposes then, it is clear that you can get more mileage out of collateral that consists of easily transferred documents. Bear this in mind as you sort through your safe deposit box. Some of those pieces of paper may be worth *money*.

If we return to the principle that you can increase your borrowing power by pledging collateral, then we can see the power the Penny Capitalist can bring to bear on the situation. If you buy something at a bargain price, it may later be used for collateral. You have increased your assets by a wise purchase, and the lending agency will recognize that fact. As an example, I bought a Navajo blanket for forty dollars and then used it as

107

collateral for a $1,000 loan. Think about that one as an example of a mechanism to transfer the risk from you to the lending agency! Also, our ranch's water shares have served as collateral; you will remember they were acquired without extra cost when the real property was purchased.

Creative Borrowing

Any capital wisely invested will provide a return in the form of income or capital gains, or both. If you have increased your investments through creative borrowing, then you are in a position to maximize your capital growth by using greater multiples provided by using others' money. Creative borrowing in its simplest sense is a technique for increasing your borrowing power beyond the overcautious limits imposed on you by a lending agency. These limits are imposed for *their* protection and for other banking reasons that have nothing to do with your goals as a Penny Capitalist. Numerous methods are available to you in your quest to increase your borrowing power.

The first step is to acquire a credit rating based on a statement of your net worth. Credit agencies are impressed if you show evidence of credit management and planning ahead. Visit with your loan officer and discuss your future investment goals with him. Don't ask for any loan at present, but indicate that when the time is ripe you will want to make certain kinds of investments. Then fill out for his files a statement of your assets, liabilities, and net worth. If you have followed my earlier prescription and acquired numerous bargains over the years at auctions, garage sales, and elsewhere, these items will beef up your net worth to a surprising degree. This evidence of thrift and wisdom on your part will impress your lender favorably. Herein lies the next opportunity for the creative borrower. The loan officer probably has no idea what your Chinese porcelains, or cloisonné, or Indian baskets are worth. He will therefore accept your appraisal unless it seems totally excessive. This situation provides the opportunity for you to gently increase your net worth.

What I am trying to point out here is that you should recognize that both you and the lender are playing a game. He doesn't care what you are really worth; all he wants is something on paper that provides evidence that he made the prudent decision. If later events turn out badly, he can always point to your statement of net worth and say, "Any loan officer would have done what I did." Suppose you picked up a rare piece of Russian vertu at an auction for $100. It is worth $2,000 according to a Sotheby–Parke Bernet sale catalog. You are justified in appraising its value at $2,000 in your statement of assets. You know, and the banker may know, that finding a buyer at that price is like finding hen's teeth, but he will probably let your valuation stand. If not, then be prepared to show him the sale catalog. You are probably worth more than you think. Some typical categories in a statement of assets and liabilities are:

Assets	Liabilities
Real Estate	**Mortgages**
Homes	Homes
Other	Other
Cash	**Current Bills**
Savings accounts	Medical
Checking accounts	Charge accounts
Savings bonds	Rent
Accounts receivable	Utilities
	Alimony
Marketable Securities	Other
Stocks	**Unpaid Taxes**
Bonds	
Other	Property
	Federal
	State
Personal Property	Local
Home furnishings	
Clothing, furs	**Debts to Individuals**
Jewelry	
Automobiles	**Cosigned Notes**
Art, antiques	

Assets	Liabilities
Collections	Installment Debts
Livestock	Auto loans
Musical instruments	Home improvement loans
Equipment	Personal loans
	Other
Long-Term Assets	
Insurance	
Annuities	
Pensions	
Benefits	
Patents	
Royalties	
Business interests	

When you fill out such a list of assets and liabilities, the final net worth usually stacks up as an agreeable surprise. You may not be rich, but you are probably a lot better off than bankrupt, and very likely better off than you thought. Furthermore, you probably have greater borrowing potential than you thought. It is possible to borrow on life insurance, on annuities, shares of stock, or even on future nonsalary earnings. When my textbook was published, I went to the bank and established a line of credit. I used as collateral the textbook contract, which promised a percentage of future sales as royalties. The contract had resided in my safe deposit box, and I had not regarded it as collateral. However when the book was actually published, I could show it to the loan officer and give him a verbal report on sales. I simply assigned the royalties to the bank and they advanced funds against the future receipt of royalties. No royalties have been paid yet, but meanwhile I have borrowed $10,000 of the bank's money, which I have invested. These investments provide further collateral in case the book royalties are disappointing. The important fact here is you too may have "forgotten" pieces of paper in your bank vault that can be used as collateral.

A while back, we established a line of credit for our cattle business. We had been raising cattle for five years beginning, as you know, by borrowing 100 percent of our initial investment. We now have a $50,000 line of credit at the bank to buy more cattle. We first established that we knew how to manage a cattle operation. We developed a herd that was both valuable and not mortgaged. We then submitted to the bank a statement of net worth plus an outline of our future plan for purchasing and then selling cattle for profit. The animals purchased would provide collateral for the funds advanced. Therefore we could simultaneously increase our collateral to match our increased borrowing. This step-by-step approach has advanced our credit rating far beyond our expectations of only a few years ago.

Increasing your borrowing ability is easier than you think. One major inexpensive step in increasing the amount of your estate is the purchase of life insurance. Term insurance is the best buy; other forms tend to divert your resources into low-paying fixed-income securities, which you as an aggressive Penny Capitalist wish to avoid like the plague. However, the purchase of term insurance can guarantee that your mortgages will be paid off in the event that something dreadful happens to you. The cost is low, and the security and peace of mind provided your family is immense. Meanwhile, you only pay premiums on the insurance you need to be covered while you are in the capital-building stage. Once you have acquired your capital you can reappraise your life insurance needs. Even if you are heavily overborrowed, the insurance provides a form of psychological support that you can't do without.

At times I have borrowed to a level of between three and four times my annual salary. This requires pretty fast footwork; it is creative borrowing at its zenith. One technique is to deal with more than one lender. At present, I have loans at three commercial banks, one agricultural lender, and a credit union. Developing this diversification will permit you to borrow from one bank to pay off a note due at another bank. (When you do this, you haven't changed your total indebtedness, but you have maintained your credit rating by paying off a note when due.) You will also have the freedom to get the best deal by comparative shopping. As a bonus, believe it or not, if you discuss a loan with a bank and then don't borrow, it's taken to mean that you are being cautious, when in fact you may simply feel the bank's terms aren't good enough. A banker equates caution with wisdom, so you are given credit you don't actually deserve.

A further step that can increase your borrowing ability is getting the seller to carry part of the amount borrowed on a mortgage. In the case of a first mortgage, you need no approval of any type from your banker. If the seller carries a second mortgage, the lending agency is often content to look out only for its own interests. If a lender has a first mortgage on 50 percent of the appraised valuation, he feels relatively safe and doesn't worry about the risk the holder of the second mortgage assumes.

Other sources of credit include various federal-agency loans. There are farm, VA, FHA, HUD, and other types of loans guaranteed by federal agencies for the purchase of real estate. There are federal loans to provide relief from natural disasters. There is one type of federal loan under the Farmers Home Administration that you cannot qualify for unless (1) you can prove that you can't survive financially on your present-sized farm, and (2) you can demonstrate that you are such a poor credit risk your local commercial bank has turned down your application. In other words, if you can't make a go of it and have no prospects of making it, Uncle Sam will bail you out at a ridiculously low interest rate! There is the Production Credit Association, which will provide money to plant crops or buy livestock. The Soil Conservation Service will cost-share on the construction of ponds, land leveling, or terracing. The Small Business Administration will provide a loan to help you start a small factory. There is even a federal agency that will loan you funds to build tourist facilities in foreign countries. The typical home-improvement loan is also federally guaranteed. You could even get an education loan and use it for investment purposes. Many of these programs include provisions that place them in the category of subsidies or even outright giveaways. While they are loans, their terms are for a long period of time, or feature a very low interest rate, or include provisions for forgiving part of the amount borrowed, or have interest-free periods; all of which should appeal to you, the Penny Capitalist. The other principal type of federal interest-free "loan" has to do with tax write-offs and how they affect your capital accumulation; I will discuss this later.

In creative borrowing the secret is not the acquisition of credit. That's easy; in fact it is too easy in our society to become overburdened with consumer credit. What is required is the acumen to borrow as much as possible for investment purposes while committing as little as possible of your take-home pay to monthly payments. My friend, the Apartment Pyramider, has done this in nifty fashion by either selling at a profit every six months or raising the rent and refinancing. One of the advantages of this game, when played to perfection, is that buyers are often attracted to the credit terms that you have been able to arrange. Thus creative borrowing adds to the ease of making a sale. Finally, and this item should be in large print, repeat, LARGE PRINT: *Funds acquired by refinancing are nontaxable* because you have technically increased your debt, rather than taken a profit!

How to Buffalo Your Banker

Let us return for a moment to the relationship between you and your loan officer. Most loans of any size are secured by collateral. Collateral, we have determined, is anything of value or a believable estimate of future earnings. A lender doesn't really want your piano or the collection of art glass you inherited from your aunt. All he wants is an assurance that you will pay the principal borrowed plus interest according to the time schedule you have agreed to. This fact means that your strongest ally is your lender. If you can't meet the terms of a loan, go to him sooner, rather than later, and work out a new arrangement. Frequently he will postpone payment of any principal as long as you can show good faith by paying the interest. This demonstrates that repossession is as abhorrent to the lender as it is to the borrower in default. Since repossession is the last thing a lender has in mind, he has only limited power to renegotiate once he has made the original loan. While you don't want to abuse this situation, it does provide some leeway in case a deal that you had arranged happens to fall through. Too many people throw in the towel and call their banker to come and repossess something simply because they feel the situation is hopeless, and they also believe that their hard-hearted banker won't give them an extension of time. Here I believe the secretiveness of bankers works to their ultimate disadvantage.

Another concern is how to find a compatible banker in the first place. Selecting a banker is analogous to picking mushrooms in the dark; you can't tell a toadstool when you find one. Bankers just sit there and smile and speak softly. You can't tell what they are thinking. You are on the defensive and they know it, which makes it even more difficult to establish a working relationship. Furthermore, and this seems to me unethical, they never tell you on what basis they decide to approve or deny loans.

Financial writer Kathryn Greene has suggested the following rules: (1) Avoid naming a figure when the banker asks how much you need. Tell him you are seeking his advice and counsel on that point. (2) Deal with the highest ranking official you can, preferably the president, but in no case below a vice-president. (3) If your request is for a business loan, insist that the banker visit your operation to see for himself what your financial needs and opportunities are. Following these suggestions will place you and your banker on the same side, working together to determine your needs. After he has appraised your situation and suggested a figure it will be difficult for him to back out. Further, he may have to defend his recommendation before a loan committee, and if it is *his* recommendation on the line, he will be more vigorous in its defense. Such tactics could even work in obtaining a loan to consolidate outstanding debts, buy a car, or make some other purchase. What you should seek is to get your banker to shift from the role of judge to that of counselor.

Meanwhile, back to choosing your banker. Banks seem to have some obscure medieval method of assigning someone to handle your account. Your "personal" banker may be a nice guy, as mine is, or he may be totally unsuited in personality to deal with your needs. In any case, you didn't select him and probably he didn't select you. More likely, he just happened to be on the floor at his desk when you walked in. If he had been out for coffee, you would have gotten someone else. How much better it would be for a bank to have a counselor who would interview all new customers and then match the interests of those customers with the capabilities of their bankers. After

114

all, it is to the bank's interest to do so if you are to become a long-term customer.

The Amortization Ripoff

We have previously discussed how a lending institution plays the game by insisting that you, the borrower, risk all of your capital while it holds a lien on the collateral to protect its part of the deal. Another aspect of borrowing money that is little understood is the relationship between the amount you borrow and the amount you pay back. A recent article in the *Wall Street Journal* documented the fact that the average home today is priced at $40,000 but that by the time it is paid for it has cost $100,000 because of the interest charges. Interest charges are not only high, they are unfairly distributed in time, with the major portion of the interest due in the early years of a mortgage and repayment of most of the principal postponed until late in the loan. The normal rate of repayment is bad enough, but if you refinance, you never get anywhere in paying off the principal. This is why the Apartment Pyramider sells after refinancing. It is the only way he can bail out with cash in hand.

Perhaps the best way to expose this loaded situation is the example amortization schedule on the following page (Schulman 1971, pp. 74–80). The schedule is set up to repay a $10,000 loan over a twenty-year term at an interest rate of 9.5 percent and shows payments by year.

The total interest paid is $12,372.65. The amount of interest paid is not unreasonable because it is computed at current rates, and these are the rates that the person taking out the mortgage agrees to pay. At least the borrower has the option of looking elsewhere for a cheaper interest rate. What is unreasonable is that the majority of the interest is paid out in the early years of the mortgage. Since most home mortgages are refinanced about every five or six years (because of ownership turnover), the lending agencies are recovering enormous amounts of interest by such a practice. In our example, it takes fourteen years, more than two-thirds of the mortgage term, before the principal payments exceed the interest payments.

Year	Interest	Principal
1	$942.46	$ 176.06
2	924.99	193.53
3	905.79	212.73
4	884.68	233.84
5	861.46	257.06
6	835.94	282.58
7	807.91	310.61
8	777.07	341.05
9	743.18	375.34
10	705.96	412.56
11	665.00	453.52
12	619.98	498.54
13	570.52	548.00
14	516.12	602.40
15	456.32	662.20
16	390.62	727.90
17	318.37	800.15
18	238.94	879.58
19	151.65	966.87
20	55.69	1,065.08

Surely this is a better deal for lenders than it is for the mortgage payer.

A more equitable system would be for interest and principal payments to be constant for each year of a mortgage term. In our example, such a plan would require $618.63 a year in interest payments plus $500 a year in principal payments. Consider the difference: after five years under current practice the owner has only $1,073.22 accumulated equity; under my plan he would have $2,500.

Carrying our analysis further, we see that, under current practice, after five years $4,519.38 interest has been paid. If at this point the property is sold and refinanced, the homeowner has paid one-third of the total twenty-year interest charge, whereas only one-fourth of the twenty-year term has elapsed. At the same time, he has accumulated only *one-tenth* of the twenty-year potential equity.

Viewed in this context, it makes ultimate sense to *assume* an existing mortgage whenever possible. This is the only way you can build equity rapidly and at the same time keep your monthly mortgage payment at a level you can afford. If you can't assume an existing mortgage because of the generally higher down payments required, then you must shop for one of the low-down-payment deals. While they penalize you in terms of interest (which, at least, is tax-deductible), they do permit you to stop paying rent and become an equity owner.

How to Print Your Own Credit

Now we come to the ultimate in creative borrowing. This is printing corporate stock for an offering to the buying public. Herein lies an opportunity to generate enormous amounts of credit at little expense; after all, it doesn't really cost very much to run a printing press. In addition, the lender (purchaser of your stock) is only guaranteed a return if your corporation makes a profit. In this type of deal the lender assumes all the risk, and the borrower is home free.

One of the best examples of this kind of situation that I know of concerns the Oceanic Exploration Company. The geologist friend to whom I sold those books some pages back had done consulting for this firm in exchange for shares of stock and knew the inside story. The company was soon to make a public offering of its stock, and he said I could get in on the ground floor. (Yep, only I was so dumb as to look for real value!)

Oceanic Exploration prospects for oil on the continental shelves of the world. In order to do this, it has acquired a large number of offshore concessions from small or new govern- ments. These are former British crown colonies and other self- governing microscopic-sized nations. When I first read the pro- spectus I thought I was reading *Scott's Postage Stamp Catalogue!* I did pick up from the prospectus that the company had found no oil, although it had a share in an interest being drilled off Ghana by another company. Further, about 90 percent of the stock was owned by the company president and his wife. A final little difficulty was that current operating expenses ex- ceeded income by a cool $700,000.

When the stock went public at ten dollars a share, I didn't

buy any. However, the act of going public made multimillionaires—on paper—of the company president and his wife since their million-plus shares were now worth at least ten dollars each. The next bit of news was that Oceanic Exploration was drilling on its concessions off the coast of Greece. When a trace of oil was reported, the stock went up to thirty dollars. At that point I suggested to my geologist mentor that he might sell out his shares because the next move might be that the company president and his wife would convert their paper fortune to real dollars by selling out. I don't know what my friend did. I don't know what the company president did. I do know that the stock price rapidly declined to around ten dollars a share following the announcement that the oil found in Greece was present only in noncommercial quantities. Here was the classic opportunity to print credit that could have been converted to real dollars at no obligation to the printer to repay anything. This is creative borrowing at its zenith.

Creative Borrowing, the Poor Man's Friend

Creative borrowing in action is simply using the system to your advantage in your drive to increase capital. The opposite type of borrowing, which, unfortunately, is practiced by most people, is borrowing out of fear. The borrower feels like a victim of the system rather than its master. He views the paying of interest as an expense to be charged against his take-home pay. A better view is to consider interest costs as a necessary expense of investment—a cost which, if the investment is wise, will be met out of increased revenues.

Briefly, these are the rules of creative borrowing, which differ to some degree from standard practice, at least as viewed from the perspective of the lending agencies:

- Creative borrowing increases your leverage; borrow as much as possible in order to multiply your equity holdings.

- Shop for the best terms in a loan. It may be the terms are more important to you than the interest rate.

- Look for the lender that specializes in the type of loan you need. Don't overlook the seller as a source of easy credit.

- Shop for the lowest interest rate.

- Make out your credit application sooner rather than later.

- Get to know your lender.

- Refinance frequently in order to consolidate loans and free up take-home pay or to reduce your interest charges.

- Learn to distinguish collateral from worthless paper.

- Learn to increase your borrowing power by maximizing your net worth on your credit application.

- Increase your borrowing power and flexibility by utilizing several lending agencies. Set your own limits as to how much you will borrow rather than letting the lender do it for you.

- Manage your credit rather than letting it manage you. Remember, you have to pay it all back plus interest, so be sure you invest wisely.

8

Playing the Market

Much has been written about the psychology of the market, when to buy and when to sell. Briefly stated, the time to buy is when you perceive real value at a bargain price. I have already covered that. The time to sell is when you can sell at a profit. It sounds easy, and it is—when you do it right. There are hang-ups when you have detected real value far in advance of others. This may mean that you have to wait years for the market to catch up to you. Meanwhile, you have to have faith, and you have to have bought so cheaply that your carrying costs are minimal.

If what I prescribe is so simple, why isn't everyone doing it? The answer lies, I believe, in poor judgment and an inability to plan ahead for the long haul. The best example I can think of to illustrate these tendencies is the local secondhand store. Most such places are jam-full of things, most of which no one is buying. These items are either useless or overpriced. What is wrong in such a situation? First, the proprietor paid too much for most of his stock. Second, he is trying to realize an immediate profit. You can't buy something today at a price approximating retail and turn around and sell it right away at a profit. You either have to resell it at a discount or wait for a rising market to bail you out. Viewed in this context, most of the stock in the average secondhand store or antique shop represents the owners' bad buys. The good buys have already been resold at a profit. In my opinion, this analogy probably fits a lot of investment portfolios as well.

So the first step in playing the market is to buy right. The next step is more painful. If you have made a purchase only to find the real value of what you bought is less than you originally thought, sell it. Sell it at a loss if you have to, but sell it. If the value isn't there, there is no point in hanging onto it, waiting for unexpected events to come to your rescue. Normally, you can sell it soon after purchase for an amount close to what you paid. The longer you hold it, the less chance this will be the case. I had this experience when buying an antique branding iron at auction. When I got it home, it was clear that it had been faked by welding new parts onto an antique handle. I sold it at the next auction at a 10 percent loss.

Selling is actually easy. What bothers most people is that selling at a loss is proof that their judgment was bad. Rather than face this unpleasant fact, they hang onto what they have, hoping against hope that something will happen to bail them out.

I have sold things of value at a price below their true worth. In some of these cases I sold too soon, in others I sold at the wrong place; the right buyers simply weren't there. My rule of thumb is: If you sold at a profit, why worry? A second rule is: A sale is a transaction. For example, suppose you see an item priced at retail in a store and you own an item of the same kind. Don't expect to sell it for the retail price. Sell it at the best price you can get. You have thereby concluded a transaction. Meanwhile, the item you saw in the store, priced higher, is probably still there, unsold.

There are two kinds of selling. The first type of sale is really an investment decision. It involves choosing the time to sell something you have invested in, in order to maximize your profit, protect your profit, or limit your losses. Properly speaking, this type of selling is an integral part of the investment process, and you must master it to do well as an investor. Frequently it is, properly speaking, an application of timing in judging market action. Often such a sale can be effected simply by calling your broker. If what you own can be sold on the securities market, the sale can be immediate and effortless. If what you have to sell is real estate, your sale will take much longer, since it must be listed, advertised, and shown, a buyer must be located, a sales contract must be drawn up, financing must be arranged, and, finally, all last-minute details must be taken care of in a closing. The entire process can easily take a year, and normally, you will need help from a broker, a mortgage banker, a lawyer, and a title company.

The other type of selling involves locating a buyer on your own. Frequently this is your only course of action when what you have to sell is an offbeat item that you either cannot or do not want to consign at auction. In this chapter I will discuss both types of selling in some detail.

Hitting High C

Setting a price according to an appraisal of the market or consultation of a price guide is no guarantee that any buyers where you live will be willing to buy at that price. Don't always try to hit the highest note; set your price so you have downward price flexibility. If you are asking twenty-five and someone offers you twenty, take it if you can make a profit at that price. If you don't take the offer, it may be months or years before the next buyer comes along. How sweet it is to be sold out in an active market, and how agonizing it is to be overstocked in a declining or inactive market. On the other hand, if the item has truly outstanding real value, you may not wish to lower your price to make a sale because you know that over time the market value is going to move up. Every transaction is different and has to be separately appraised.

Everyone is looking for a bargain. To put it in other terms, no one wants to pay retail price, for everyone believes that is evidence he has been taken. Therefore, set your price so your buyers can go away congratulating themselves on making a good buy. If you can do that and still show a profit, they will be back to buy again at a later date, and you will still be in business. Of course some buyers are unrealistic and you have to turn down their ridiculous offers, but I am not referring to them. As an example of what I mean, we have sold some of the beef we raised on our ranch. Our customers have paid an average of thirty cents a pound less for our packaged product than they would pay in a store. Nonetheless, they expect the meat to be of identical quality to that priced higher. When we provide such a product, we have stroked their egos. They are pleased to buy from us because we are helping them demonstrate what shrewd shoppers they are.

I have stated that it is unrealistic to expect to buy at today's prices, immediately mark up the item, and resell it quickly at a profit. This is what most people try to do. As a successful Penny Capitalist you should expect to hold onto what you have for some time before the market has adjusted to a new price level. In other words, true investing normally is for the long haul. In some instances the situation can dramatically change in a short period of time (such as the increase in the price of gold and silver since we bought our mineralized mountain land). Nonetheless, few investments can be made in the *expectation* of a quick and profitable resale. Even in an up market the commissions you have to pay brokers may well wipe out any short-term gain over a period of a year or less. If you made good buys in the first place, there is little risk in holding on for the long pull. Usually, in fact, the longer you hold on, the greater is your built-in increase in value. If you don't wish to sell at present, you can frequently use the equity in your investment for collateral and borrow against its increased value.

Another major selling rule is: Don't hold out for top dollar. Today's price may be the highest price you will ever see, so don't pass up a sale today hoping for something better tomorrow. As an example, I can cite the cattle market. Cattle prices are either bad or fairly good. They are almost never excellent, or at least, they have only been excellent once in the past twenty years. The moment that prices begin to look good to the producer of cattle there are powerful forces that swing into action to bring those prices down. These include the packers, the retail stores, the consumers, and even the federal government. So when prices for cattle *begin* to look good, I sell; almost certainly the next event will be that prices go down rather than increase further.

Selling Against the Trend

Often selling must be carried out in the face of contrary opinion. A series of brokerage-house recommendations concerning

Occidental Petroleum (OXY) can illustrate this principle (Scheinman 1970, pp. 170–72).

1. July 3, 1968—51⅞. Since early June OXY has been backing and filling between 50 and 55 [dollars a share] while volume has lightened considerably. This performance suggests the stock is undergoing nothing more than a normal profit taking phase, and that its intermediate to longer term uptrend remains intact. Consequently, we would be inclined to take advantage of the current dip to add to previous commitments. We are raising our short-term objective to 63–65.

2. August 2, 1968—44⅞. With OXY having fulfilled the downside projection from the minor top pattern traced in June and July, with apparent technical support indicated just below current quotations, and with the stock's price having returned to its major trendline, purchase of OXY is recommended for a trend objective of 69–70.

3. September 10, 1968—44. With an aggressive, intelligent management team backed by rapidly rising earnings, Occidental's capacity for further growth remains substantial and the stock, we believe, will prove a profitable addition to portfolios geared for appreciation.

4. November 15, 1968—47⅞. OXY's record of growth and development during the last decade has been seldom equalled by any company in the history of American industry. The common stock appears attractively priced for longer term enhancement of capital.

5. December 9, 1968—47. The growth of Occidental during the past ten years is almost legendary and illustrates what is possible when a company follows an aggressive forward-looking approach to corporate evolution. . . . The shares are considered to offer potential for above-average long term capital appreciation.

6. January 14, 1969—45. Contrary to some thought now prevalent that OXY is "through" as an investment, we are taking this opportunity to re-recommend the stock as a highly desirable vehicle for inclusion in capital-gains-oriented portfolios. . . . Upside price potential can be targeted at 60 plus over a 6–9 month period.
7. March 17, 1969—42. Despite the weakening action of the market in general, Occidental Petroleum seems an attractive investment for aggressive individuals seeking appreciation.

According to Scheinman (1970, p. 172), what was actually happening at this time was a massive dispersal of OXY stock by sophisticated investors to uninformed investors who were brainwashed by a bullish investment press. The correct investment action in this situation was to do the opposite of what the brokerage houses were recommending.

OXY continued to slide, and later that same year when it reached 28, on the advice of my broker, I got in on the action. I was naïve, as I believed that at approximately one-half of its recent high, OXY was a bargain. The underlying problems were still unknown to the general investing public, and sophisticated selling pressure continued. The price continued to slide, and at 15 I bought some more shares, which lowered my average cost per share to about 22. For awhile it sank even lower, and then, on good news, rapidly advanced above 20. I phoned in a sell order to my broker at 23. A day or two later the price was hovering around 22½, so I phoned the broker and told him to sell it at the market price. The price has never been as high since.* In fact, most of the time since then the price has ranged from 9 to 14.

Why did I sell when I did? Well, I am not sure, except that the price stopped going up. I *revised* my estimate of what was an achievable price and sold at the going market price. By doing

---

* This was written in 1976. In 1977 OXY went to 30 briefly. It is now back to about 22.

this I didn't get locked into the psychological trap of staying fixed on a certain price no matter what the market did. I was also lucky but that's a part of investing too. You can expect some good luck occasionally if you own something. If you don't own anything, luck doesn't matter anyway. Joseph Kennedy once said that the reason for his success was "selling too soon." He is right for more than one reason. The market may *not* go higher. Even if it does, the demand at the top may be very thin, and something that was in great demand at a few dollars lower will take much longer to sell because buyers are in short supply.

The OXY situation and my participation in it demonstrates several major selling principles. (1) Just because something is selling at half its previous high doesn't make it automatically a bargain. The underlying factors must still be adequately understood, and in this case they weren't by the brokerage houses and their customers. (2) The selling of OXY by informed investors was carried out in the face of strong contrary opinion. The moral in this tale is to rely on your own knowledge when taking action. (3) My selling was not totally a fluke. I recognized that no matter what was influencing the short-term price of the stock, the primary factors were bearish. I sold on a rally and sold at the market. My market stop-price seemed unrealistic the day after I called it in, so I revised my sell order to "sell at the market." The selling principle I employed was: Don't become wedded to a specific price; revise your opinion as soon as you have new data.

Dollar-Value Selling

Another technique of selling is "sell some and keep some." This frees up capital to reinvest at a later date. It also provides a hedge against higher prices. If the market moves higher, you still have an equity position. This type of approach is especially good in real estate. You sell enough of your property to recover your initial investment. What you have remaining gives you a free ride, which if an up market is in progress, may be very good indeed.

Eric Emory has developed a variant of this technique that he terms "dollar-value selling" (Emory 1973). When your stock portfolio exceeds a certain value, you sell across the board enough stock to reduce the total value of the remaining portfolio to the desired level. You keep the realized cash in an interest-bearing account, where you have it in reserve for future buying opportunities. If the portfolio value drops below your established level, you buy in to restore the value to that level. Emory claims his method yields results in excess of buying the market averages.

One aspect of dollar-value selling is that you make decisions to sell as part of your overall investment strategy. This avoids the common pitfall of becoming concerned that you sold out too cheap. Most people try to hang on to get the top dollar, only to end up missing the top of the market altogether. A consistent selling plan avoids this. Further, when you sell something you have made a transaction. I never look back and say that I should have done so and so. I accept what I received and move on to the next transaction. Even if the price moved higher and I could have sold for more, I have no regrets. All that counts is to show a profit in the long run. At the same time, I am fully aware that it is possible to sell too soon. The key to the situation is to properly appraise the market on a continuing basis. Hold your investments as long as you can tell that the market is heading higher. When it slows, sell. Playing any market involves constant reappraisal to determine whether at current prices there is a reasonable expectation of higher prices in the future. A trap to avoid is the fixing of a price in your mind. Something may be "worth X amount," but if you can't find someone willing to pay that much, then such a price is meaningless.

Mathematical Selling

Part of the wisdom applied to selling is in knowing what you have and then developing a marketing plan. Louis Rukeyser (1974, pp. 135–44) covers this aspect in great detail. He discusses the mathematical approach to selling in which (in the organized securities market) you place a stop-loss order, which instructs your broker to sell your stock if the price falls to a certain level that you specify. If your order is 10 percent below the recent high price then presumably this order provides safety if the stock should plunge downward. Presumably your stop-loss order will protect most of your paper profits. However, if the stock should rise, you simply move your stop-loss point upward, staying 10 percent below the high.

The problem with this approach is that your stock may rebound; meanwhile, you have been automatically sold out and you watch the rest of the action from the sidelines. This happened to me with some Kaiser Aluminum stock that I owned. My stop-loss order sold me out one-half a point (fifty cents) above the rebound level. Since then, I have learned that part of my problem was that my stop-loss order was placed at an even number. Probably lots of others had picked the same point. When the price was near that magic number, the Kaiser Aluminum specialists sold their holdings, driving the price temporarily lower and forcing the sales at the stop-loss price. They then bought back in and could profit on the ensuing rise.

The supposed advantage of the mathematical approach to selling is that it permits you to take most of your profits and close out your positions in an unemotional, businesslike way. Critics of the approach, and these include Rukeyser, note that by doing so you may well miss out on the future great rise of a spectacular growth stock. Rukeyser's advice is to reappraise your stock constantly for evidence that the continued growth potential is there. If it is, hang on, even in the face of a temporary downturn. He cites evidence of fund managers taking what they believed to be good profits on Xerox only to sit idly by later and watch the price go up and up and up.

Proper Timing Is Infinitely Better than 20/20 Hindsight

Proper timing is the major feature of a successful transaction. To buy just prior to an upward price move and sell prior to a price retreat is everyone's goal. The actual success ratio of most investors in this endeavor is rather low.

My primary concern here is to point out that most price moves, when they occur, tend to be rapid and of short duration.

You must make your buy-and-sell decisions in advance of such moves because once they begin the action may be too rapid for you to buy in or sell out with a reasonable degree of safety. In other words, buying and selling during price moves puts you in the category of the day-trader. It puts you in competition with the professional traders, at a competitive disadvantage. On the other hand, proper timing puts you in the right position prior to the price move. What can happen if your timing is off is that you buy near the top or sell out near the bottom, and then you have to wait a full market cycle before your funds may again be gainfully employed. In short, improper timing leads you into long intervals in which either the market moves against you or moves sideways. During such intervals your funds would be working at a better advantage if they were somewhere else. An interest-bearing account or bond is infinitely better than a market position when the market is moving against you.

All of this discourse is analogous to pointing out that poison is bad for you. The meaningful question is, How can you time your market decisions to take advantage of price moves?

My advice is to analyze the market on three different levels of abstraction. What is the relationship between the current market situation and its long-term history? What is the recent history of the market? What is the history of price movements in your particular item of interest? These patterns may well give you some indications as to where the market is headed. In analyzing the stock market I study the trends by reading the *Barron's* and *Wall Street Journal* assessments about once a month. This gives me an updated impression of market trends. If I read such articles on a daily basis I tend merely to become confused.

Be prepared for those times when your reading leads you to no clear impression as to the next market move. When that occurs, it is a signal that the market may well go sideways, a good time to have your funds somewhere else.

Another form of bad timing is to sell out after a price rise only to watch your selection go on up. This happened to my friend the Inheritor. Her broker got her into Burroughs and then got out with a reasonable profit. Both were chagrined when Burroughs went up another 100 points.

Idiot version of the small investor's luck in the market

Timing is only partially a result of foresight and analysis; its other component is luck. Luck is that element that causes you to either sell out or hang on without any concrete reason for doing so. Luck is that extra element that sometimes bails you out of a loser or more frequently turns a good prospect, that you properly analyzed, into a real winner. You may identify an undervalued property and buy it in anticipation of a 100 percent return on your investment. Meanwhile, if the entire market in that item moves to higher ground enabling you to clear 1,000 percent, then that's luck. That happened to me with my Navajo blanket. When I bought it for ten dollars I knew it was a steal. Three years later it was appraised at $350, which sounded pretty good. However the market boomed up after that for the next five years at as much as 50 percent a year. My luck was in not selling at $350 and taking a reasonable profit; as you already know I eventually sold it for $2,000.

In the cattle business we recently went through two years of ruinous prices. Numerous cattlemen have gone out of business simply because their costs of production exceeded the market price of their product. During this period purebred animals that sold at auction in 1972 for $1,000 a head were resold in 1974 for $200, and these were the very same animals! The glimmer of better times ahead began in 1975. By 1976 most people were still in the dumps mentally, but a few could see beyond the immediate present. At this time, we signed a contract to buy calves for future delivery. The price was the February 1976 price, but delivery dates were May 1976, October 1976, May 1977, and October 1977.

Prices have already improved, and we sold some of the first-delivery calves in June 1976 at a profit. We are not home scot-free yet, as we have a firm contract to buy all those calves at our agreed-upon price no matter what the market does. However if our timing was right, and so far all signs are encouraging, then we could be selling calves next year at a 50 to 100 percent profit.

The point here is that timing was the essence of this investment decision. We waited out the bottom of the market and then, when most people were still overcome with negativism, we bought in. I might add that a further reason for our decision was the fact that the securities market had already moved up.

In other words, we had corroborative evidence that the economy in general was recovering. Meanwhile, the cattle market was lagging behind the general economy somewhat, and that made it seem to be a bargain.

Timing in selling is equally important. However another element enters in here. Selling decisions are not made simply on the basis of market conditions. Equally important is the carrying costs you have in order to maintain your investment. If you are paying interest, maintenance costs, etc., then hanging on may not pay off. If you are backed into such a corner, the best timing is probably selling sooner in order to limit your potential losses. In short, proper timing may be learned, but it is more an art than a science.

You Can Sell Anything. Or Don't Throw It Away—Some Idiot May Buy It!

I have been amazed over the years to observe that you can sell anything. As evidence of this, consider the antics of Churchy and Uncle Baldwin in the accompanying cartoon as they plot to get rich by supplying the missing ingredient every housewife needs. The machinations of Pogo's friends notwithstanding, the best example that I know personally of selling something totally worthless concerns an old coffeepot of blue graniteware. It was smashed flat and shot full of holes. As a joke, I slipped it into the Antique Lady's box of antiques. She didn't find it until she got home the next day. Undaunted, she advertised it as a relic of the Civil War battlefield at Glorieta, New Mexico, and sold it for five bucks!

While dismantling an old piano for the wood, I removed a small tin plate from around the pedals. Painted black, the plate carried the gold-lettered legend "Mouse Proof" and the date "1893." The purpose of the plate was to prevent mice from invading the piano through the holes for the pedals. The tin plate was absolutely useless, but it did look like an antique and it was dated. I sold it to the Antique Lady for a dollar just to prove that I could sell it. She didn't know what to do with it either, but bought it anyway because it was a "bargain."

When we bought our pasture land, we inherited fences that

Churchy and Uncle Baldwin decide to sell dirt.

were about seventy years old. The wooden fence posts were rotted off at the base and most of them were held up by the wire. We put up new fencing with steel posts. Since the wooden posts were too short they were no longer serviceable as fence posts. However I advertised them as suitable for wood-carving and decorative patio fences. I sold several pickup loads at two dollars a post. Meanwhile I had only paid $1.25 each for the new steel posts. At this point my father-in-law was really impressed. He said that if I could sell rotten old fence posts, selling iceboxes to Eskimos was nothing.

Finding the Right Buyer

Holding for the long term may not be a plan, just the only alternative you have. One aspect of selling is holding until the market reappraises what you have. Often there is no organized market, and you couldn't sell what you have if you wanted to. So you just sit and hold. I did this with the geology books I mentioned earlier. I currently hold about five hundred 78-rpm records and radio transcriptions that I bought in 1950. There is no organized market for these, so I am holding them until buyer interest picks up. They are costing me nothing to hold. I also have hundreds of feet of antique barbed wire that we removed when we replaced our fences. Someday someone will want it and be willing to pay an attractive price.

Selling involves three basic principles: (1) selling at the right time, (2) selling at a price buyers will find attractive, and (3) selling to the right buyer.

More people than you might think believe that price-cutting is the secret to selling. Actually, what you have to sell may only appeal to a few buyers. However, when you locate such a buyer, he may be eager to buy and price is no obstacle.

Finding the right buyer, then, involves finding someone who appreciates what you have as much as you do. For example, my friend the Fastest Trader in the West offered me an original oil painting of Indian dancers. It was painted by a known Indian artist, and the work was signed and dated. I wasn't really interested in the painting for myself, so I turned him down. A few days later he offered it again at 50 percent off his original price. At that price it was a bargain, and the Antique Lady bought it. The painting was shown to one buyer two weeks later, and it sold at a 237 percent markup.

Several basic principles are illustrated by this example. The original price offered by my trader friend was not unreasonable. He simply had failed to locate the right buyer. The right buyer was not your everyday TV watcher; in fact the right buyer was a rare bird. What happened was that the Antique Lady knew that a certain museum collected modern Indian paintings and that they had a budget for acquisitions. Once the museum saw the painting the sale was easy, as they knew what they wanted and could appreciate the painting on its own terms. From their point of view the real value was there.

Selling also involves matching the quantity of the item offered to the strength of the market. Occasionally, items of great rarity come on the market in large collections that are being dispersed from estates. The dumping of the entire collection could well break the price level. A prudent dispersal involves selling the collection little by little over a period of time. Even better is making the dispersal at a series of sales in different regions.

Selling also involves matching what you have for sale with buyer interest. The Antique Lady recently said that she can't give silverplate away, either flatware or serving dishes. There simply is no market at any price. She couldn't understand this because sterling pieces are already so expensive that people can't afford them. She plans to pack up her silverplate and simply wait until the market changes and silverplate comes into demand. Viewed in this context, now is a good time to accumulate silver plate; it is also a poor time to sell silverplate owing to a lack of buyer interest. This situation fits one of the great rules of investing: things vary in popularity over time. Art dealers understand this principle very well, and their storerooms are full of paintings of schools that are currently out of favor. When one of these schools is reappraised by art historians, buyer interest is stimulated and the paintings move out of storage and are placed on display in the galleries.

Another basic rule is that whatever is in vogue and commanding high prices today probably will be out of vogue and selling lower at sometime in the future. An exception to this rule is the art market. Powerful forces coincide to keep up art prices. Items placed in collections are temporarily off the market and thus tend to increase the prices of those items that are offered for sale. Museums enter the market as buyers, and most of what they buy is permanently removed from the market. Thus the available supply of works by specific artists is both limited and steadily diminishing. The provision of a tax exemption for gifts to museums also steadily decreases the supply. Therefore, even though some schools of art may be currently out of vogue, their prices are more apt to rise steadily rather than to decline, owing to the counterbalancing effect of the steady reduction in supply. There are some exceptions, such as the eighteenth century English portraitists, whose works reached their peak price levels in the 1920s and have not regained those heights since. However, in general, even in the art market you should conform to the rule that when prices are high or rising, sell, and when prices are falling or stable, buy.

Barter, Selling on Commission, and Other Gambits

Our income tax structure is based on the receipt of cash for services or the documented receipt of cash for goods; that is, the paying of income taxes is based on a percentage of the income for which documentation exists. Normally such documentation is kept by the employer, so the employee has little to do with the entire process. As you know, the majority of all taxes are collected by means of withholding them directly from employees' pay.

In recent years I have noticed an increasing number of people reverting to barter as a means to augment their income. They exchange goods or services for other goods or services. The advantages are twofold. In the first place, they have thus located a market for either their leisure-time services or their surplus goods. In the second place, such an exchange results in the avoidance of taxes by both parties. The even exchange of goods results in the avoidance of any capital gains tax.

To state our Penny Capitalist law for this section: $1.00 kept from the IRS through barter exchange is worth $1.25 earned and taxable. To my knowledge there are no studies that document the extent of barter in America today. It would be interesting to obtain such figures; I am sure they would be higher than anyone realizes. If I were to guess, I would say that about one out of every three Americans is engaged in the barter system to some degree or another. I know of examples of trading refinished furniture for piano lessons, beef for hay baling, Navajo rugs for silver and turquoise jewelry, etc. There is even a local store that deals in Indian crafts and new musical instruments. Therefore you can trade old Navajo rugs for a new electric guitar! If you have a capital gain in those rugs, no one would ever know. Daily labor such as stone-laying, plumbing, electrical work, and such are often exchanged by professionals in their spare time for car repair, sports equipment, food, and whatnot. Even doctors, lawyers, and dentists will barter their services; give it a try!

To my way of thinking the increase in barter has social and economic significance from two points of view. First, as I have mentioned, it avoids taxation. Second, and perhaps more important, those exchanging their services for goods would rather have their ownership tied up in goods than in currency because they lack faith in our monetary system. They realize that no matter what our government is saying at the moment, our currency is being devalued. Meanwhile, goods, as a result of inflationary forces, are constantly increasing in cost. Remember that after the Nixon currency devaluations the official U.S. position was that the average American wouldn't be affected at all by devaluation. Ask any citizen today how he feels on that one! The average family today drives a foreign car or motorcycle, has a foreign-made camera, radio, or TV, and routinely buys numerous items made abroad, and their prices were all driven up by those devaluations. Even U.S. military suppliers buy enormous amounts of goods from foreign sources. Meanwhile, we have lost control of the world price of oil, and that factor affects the price of everything else we buy or produce. Barter, then, represents a return at the grass roots level, by the average citizen, to a primeval level of exchange where the goods or services involved are exchanged at an agreed-upon valuation acceptable to both parties.

On a slightly higher level of abstraction, garage sales may also be viewed as barter. Families sell off their surplus items and they buy other such items at other garage sales. In fact, the average garage sale sponsored by several families results in more trading between the sponsors than sales to others.

Barter provides a means for the shrewd trader to increase his equity. He may start with inexpensive items and trade up to more and more expensive ones. Meanwhile, his increase in equity has not been diluted by any assessed taxes. Eventually, he may be able to trade his stock of valuables for the equity in an income-producing property. At that time he has successfully converted from a capital-gains-building, non-income-producing situation to one that is income-producing. If he trades he may accomplish this transition tax-free. At a later date, when his situation changes, he may want to trade back the other way.

Recently we exchanged some breeding cattle for a Navajo rug. We entered the transaction in our ranch records as a sale, and therefore it became part of our 1975 ranch profits. Some people would not have kept such records. Furthermore, since then we have traded our rug equity for some bracelets because it seemed as though they might be easier to sell. The rug transaction came at a time when cash was in short supply, and if we had to find a cash buyer we might still be looking. Meanwhile the cows were eating on a daily basis, and therefore, barter seemed to be the best solution for both parties. Thus you can see that not all barter has tax avoidance as its primary goal. It can also be a means of selling something when cash is tight.

We should perhaps evaluate the significance of these factors in terms of their future potential. If barter is so widespread today and if people have so little faith in currency, what does this bode for the future? In my opinion there is the possibility that barter of goods and services may be modified to include the use of widely accepted standards of value—a true currency. If our paper currency is replaced in this role, even on a part-time basis, the items that seem reasonable to substitute would be silver bullion ("junk") coins; such coins would be widely accepted as authentic and as real repositories of value. All that is needed is their return to circulation with new values being assigned; for example, at 1978 bullion prices the average silver dollar with a common mint mark is worth five dollars. It would only take a determined minority to implement such a practice. After all, this is not the first time that inflation has made a mockery of our currency values. The phrase "not worth a Continental" refers to the valueless Continental dollar issued during and after the Revolutionary War.

Selling on commission is another excellent equity-building mechanism. If you have a friend who has several items he wishes sold, you can contact buyers and arrange for them to pay your friend directly, with you getting part of the goods offered as your commission. The beauty of this kind of arrangement is that you have none of your funds invested, only your time; for your part, it is not a cash transaction. With no funds at all invested in your "keepers," you are free to hold them for capital appreciation without any pressure whatsoever to sell, there being no carrying cost on what you have kept. If you sell them it is because you need funds for another purpose.

A refined version of this is trading commissions. You may have the world's finest Mongolian bedpan, while your friend has an extremely rare but unappreciated Iranian altar cloth. You know a prospective buyer for his altar cloth, and he for your bedpan, so you agree to sell each other's priceless items. (I don't know how the result would be viewed for tax purposes if you both were successful.)

A tax-free exchange is another gambit. The Art Dealer told me he could take in items of value on trade on valuable paintings. Such trades could be arranged to be a tax-free exchange rather than a sale on which a capital gains tax would be due.

Some real estate transactions are tax-free exchanges of like property. If this can be accomplished, you may be able to convert to a more favorable situation without having had your equity reduced through imposition of a capital gains tax. Owing to inflation such a situation is most common, as almost every property that you have held for any length of time has a built-in increase in equity due to inflation.

Investment credits are another form of equity formation not requiring actual cash. For example, there are cost-sharing projects in which your portion of the costs is made up in part by your contribution of labor or materials. Say you need lumber or rocks to complete a project and you own a suitable source; you may charge off these materials and receive a cost-sharing credit. Meanwhile, you may not have had any buyers for those same materials. In any event, I doubt that such cost-sharing credits are taxable. If you can pull off such a deal, you have converted a nonsalable item into a recognized equity and saved yourself a cash outlay at the same time.

Recently our artist neighbor finished a painting of our barn and cows. We liked it and decided to buy it from her. The final transaction was by barter. We traded some beef and odd-shaped pieces of walnut lumber for the painting. The walnut pieces were cut from a stump we salvaged and were of small and irregular form. She wanted the walnut as bases for bronze sculpture so the trade was to her advantage. Our intended use of the painting is to submit it as a cover for a cattle-breed magazine. If we are successful, we will obtain free national advertising value for our ranch that would otherwise cost at least $1,000. This is another example of a trade representing an exchange in lieu of cash. The resultant value is significant, but is not calculable directly as income and hence is not taxable.

Unloading a Bummer

Items of uncertain value pose the greatest problem for the investor at all levels. If the value of an item has been overstated through overexuberant or even fallacious publicity, its next most obvious price movement is down. There is nothing so disheartening as to buy something and then realize after more extensive examination that the real value either isn't there or has been overstated. The typical reaction is to hold on and hope that what you know in your heart is wrong and that the price will continue to go up no matter what the underlying principles. In the stock market this kind of action is called an overrun. It can occur, but it is simply a result of misdirected mass psychology. The professional investor has no business being caught up in any such euphoria.

If you have made a bad buy, there are at least several things you can do. The best course of action is to sell quickly. This is your best opportunity to recover most of your investment because the underlying negative factors may not yet be fully realized by the buying public. It is even possible that you can get out at a profit due to the existence of an overrun. A second possibility is to sell at the same place that you bought. If the item sold there at an unrealisitc price before, it may well do so again, and you can at least make back most of what you paid.

Both of these techniques assume that a market exists. There are times when it seems that no one else is as stupid as you were, and therefore you can't unload what you have at any price. At this point your best bet may be to trade what you have for someone else's white elephant. He may have something of use to you that is either of no use to him or may even represent an expense that he is unwilling to continue.

An example of this concerns my partner in the cattle business. He bought two turquoise and silver squash-blossom necklaces at auction as an investment. He paid $1,200 for the pair. When he tried to sell them, no buyers could be found. An appraisal by a local Indian trader was that these were "cheapy squashes" made with machine-stamped metal parts and treated turquoise. The trader's appraisal of their combined value was $465. At this point I suggested we trade them to the Cattle Baron for frozen semen from his prize bull. I knew that it only cost him a dollar to put up an ampule of semen, which he then sold for fifteen. Since his initial cost was low, he might be willing to trade. My partner and I discussed our trading price and decided that, at fifteen dollars an ampule, we wanted 100 ampules, but would accept 50 as our minimum price. We approached the Cattle Baron with the necklaces, but didn't state that we wanted 100 ampules in return. We simply asked what he would offer. He said that since it was a trade, he was willing to use a figure of ten dollars an ampule. We thus settled at 120 ampules, or 20 above our asking price. We then entered this transaction into our ranch partnership records. This gave my partner a tax deduction for his entire $1,200 investment instead of a $735 loss. At the same time the investment in the semen will improve the quality of our cattle, which will eventually result in higher prices. It was a good deal for the Cattle Baron too, as his cash investment in the necklaces was only $120. This is as good an example as I know of how a trade can bail one out of a bad investment.

If you can't trade your way out of a bad investment, there are two other recourses. You can write off the loss on your tax return or you can keep whatever you have on the long chance that it may eventually regain some of its prior value. In rare instances such miracles do occur. There are numerous stories of corporate stock used to paper bathroom walls later becoming valuable as the result of a mineral strike, reorganization of the company, etc. Such occurrences are rare but not unheard of. In general, it may be said that the Penny Capitalist will be more likely to hang onto something thought worthless than will the ordinary person. It may someday be worth something, and it isn't costing anything to keep. My geology books are an example of such a situation; remember, it took fifteen years before I was able to turn them at a profit.

Selling a Package

Most people try to sell on their own terms, which is usually self-defeating. After all, the buyer is the one who puts up the cash and takes the risk, so make the sales package attractive to him. If the buyer doesn't have cash, what can he trade as a down payment? What kind of time payments can he make? What interest payments are reasonable? In every sale the buyer and seller must reach a compromise position. What may be important to each varies according to the situation of each. For one it may be price or length of time payments. For the other it may be relief from payments, relief from risk, or simply the opportunity to devote more time to other interests. The sale should therefore be viewed as a package whose elements are specifically adjusted to the needs of both buyer and seller. Often the terms are more important to the buyer and seller than is the price. If you as seller seek to meet the buyer's needs rather than your own, you will be more successful. I recently sold some cattle to our neighbor. The aspect that closed the deal was that we would keep the animals for two months while he fenced his pasture. This convenience to him was crucial, whereas for us it represented little in the way of inconvenience.

Intimidation as a Selling Technique

Robert J. Ringer, a real estate salesman, has written a book called *Winning through Intimidation* (1974), which says about all there is to say on this subject. He claims that the successful salesman has to intimidate both buyer and seller in order to successfully walk away with a reasonable and earned commission. He believes intimidation is so important that it represents the difference between an adequate and fair commission versus either an inadequate commission or even no commission at all.

Ringer's approach embodies a series of steps that I will list below. What is perhaps even more important than the specific steps he recommends, is the fact that he believes that intimidation can be learned. Ringer's practices have included taking with him to important meetings a flock of secretaries armed with typewriters, calculators, copy machines, and tape recorders. Such techniques served the double purpose of performing normal recording functions and intimidating the opposition.

The rules that Ringer developed are specifically adapted to real estate, but they may be abstracted here for our use. The first rule is that success does not automatically come to him who works long and hard. A positive mental attitude is not enough; you must change the attitudes of others toward you, and that is where intimidation comes into focus. Ringer's second rule is that you can achieve a positive mental attitude by assuming that your results will be negative. This frees you from any anxiety connected with whether or not you make the sale. You assume failure, therefore you can be calm and be at your best in emphasizing the positive aspects of the sales situation. Your lack of anxiety will leave you prepared to maximize whatever sales opportunities exist. The third rule is to be prepared. Do your homework, acquire all requisite credentials, get the legal support you need, acquire any licenses or other requisites, and be prepared to go to ultimate extremes to ensure that no delays will ensue. (Ringer has even flown a secretary across the country to bring back a necessary document without delay.) The primary point is that for you to be totally prepared for any eventuality serves to intimidate those you are dealing with.

The principal steps in the actual selling process as itemized by Ringer (p. 96) include:

1) Obtain a product to sell.
2) Locate a market for the product.
3) Implement a marketing method.
4) Be able to close the sale.
5) Get Paid.

Other steps he recommends are: (1) Always work alone; others usually confuse or foul up a deal rather than helping. (2) Work only on those situations that can logically be expected to be sold. Avoid the unmakeable deal and pie-in-the-sky. (3) Get your agreement with the seller in writing. (4) Weed out the nonserious buyers. (5) Keep the buyer and seller from direct communication with each other. (6) Avoid all delays because

143

any delay tends to kill a deal. (7) When closing a deal be prepared to have to play all your cards including your legal backup. (8) When closing emphasize to the buyer and seller that other offers they have received are probably not backed by any serious intent. (This avoids the "Better Deal" syndrome in which the seller imagines that something better is just down the road.) Simultaneously, emphasize to the buyer that if he doesn't snap up this deal others will, and he will lose out.

Ringer's rules include commonsense steps in the selling process and step-by-step intimidation of the buyer and seller. If you end up in the salesman's role, try it; you will probably like it.

Selling is an art, but it is practiced according to a set of basic principles. I have outlined these principles above, but learning them is not enough. You must recognize that selling involves psychological considerations that are in basic contradiction to the personality characteristics of most individuals. If you have something that is of excellent quality and that has been assigned a high value by the public at large, sell it for the best price you can get. The average individual would buy such an item convinced that its price will go higher. Whether the price actually does go higher is irrelevant. What is important is that the seller has transferred the risk associated with holding for a higher price to the buyer, making a profit at the same time. The basic acquisitiveness of the average buyer further contributes to his unwillingness to sell at a reasonable figure. He holds on trying to hit "High C," and often sells out much later at a lower price because the market never met his expectations.

Any successful investment program must include as much emphasis on proper selling as proper buying. Inasmuch as selling requires traits contrary to the basic inclinations of most of us, it is more difficult than buying to do well. Here are the basic rules:

- Sell sooner rather than later.

- Remember that you can sell anything.

- Sell at a fair profit; don't try to get top dollar.

- Don't hold out for the top of the market.
- Don't regret selling "too soon."
- Trade what you can't sell.
- Keep what you can't sell or trade.
- Package your product. Don't insist on the full price up front; sell on time if you have to.
- Learn intimidation.

9

Repellents for the Tax Bite

The income tax laws in the United States structure our everyday life in ways too weird and wonderful to mention. All of us are familiar with the tax withholding imposed upon our paychecks. However, how many are familiar with the specific tax provisions that apply to a Subchapter S corporation, or a tax-loss carry-forward situation, depletion versus depreciation, investment tax-credit, and other such provisions of our tax code?

When you investigate each of these provisions, you will find that in the situations where they may be applied they provide relief from taxation. The rules of the game are simple: Where a tax provision is applicable, those fortunate enough to qualify for that provision pay less in taxes. It is interesting to note that a majority of these situations apply to a relatively small number of taxpayers. For example, there was a recent newspaper article citing tax relief enacted into a law so specific that it applies primarily to the Kennedy family. A tax provision enacted in 1954 stated that income from accumulation trusts that paid returns every five years would only have the income of the current year taxed. Senator Edward Kennedy currently benefits from this by having 80 percent of his annual trust income of $400,000 tax-free. Not bad, if you happen to be born a Kennedy.

It is no coincidence that most of these provisions have the support of strong lobbying groups, for they are the ones who will benefit. On the other hand, it is equally clear that the average taxpayer who subsists on the leavings from a paycheck based on his individual earning power has no opportunity to

Idiot version of taxation

utilize these tax-saving provisions because he doesn't qualify. In short, while all of the so-called tax loopholes are legal, many of them cannot be utilized by the majority of wage-earners. The latter pay a higher percentage of their income in taxes than do those blessed by the Internal Revenue Code.

A proper view of this situation is that income earned by direct personal services is penalized, whereas income earned through investments is sheltered and protected. There are those who would loudly decry this situation to be unfair and discriminatory (Stern 1973). But the system makes no pretense of being fair; as applied, it simply seeks to collect those taxes that are legally due. We as individuals may join action-oriented groups that seek to change our tax structure, but I view such actions as largely counterproductive. Instead of wasting time trying to change a system that was designed by the rich and powerful to protect the privileges of the rich and powerful, and which they will continue to support by all of the means at their disposal, I suggest that the Penny Capitalist profit by their example and seek to join them.

The tax structure as written is equitable in the sense that *everyone* who qualifies may, for instance, charge off depreciation or take an investment tax-credit. What the average taxpayer needs to do is divert more of his income into tax-reducing situations. Take a look at the accompanying two tables, which document who pays what, by income level, under our current tax laws (Stern 1973, p. 11).

Whereas the above tables may seem unduly generous to those with high incomes, the fact is that most everyone can benefit from use of tax loopholes in ways which I will document later.

A critical distinction concerns the difference between income and capital gains. Income is your earnings resulting from your own personal efforts, such as personal services, commissions, writing, or performing. Capital gains are those earnings resulting from invested capital. Capital gains are taxed at a lower rate than income. This is why we have millionaires who pay no income tax. They may pay substantial amounts of capital gains taxes because they have capital gains, but if they have no earned *income*, no income taxes are assessed. In 1975 the average taxpayer paid 20.7 percent of his income in taxes

148

Percentage of Income Paid in Tax, by Income Level

For a family with this much income . . .	this is the percent of their income that . . .		
	the tax law seems to call on them to pay in taxes	*they actually do pay in taxes after using the loopholes*	*the loopholes save them*
$2,000–$3,000	1.9%	0.5%	1.4%
$5,000–$6,000	7.5	2.8	4.7
$10,000–$11,000	12.4	7.6	4.8
$20,000–$25,000	20.8	12.1	8.7
$75,000–$100,000	46.0	26.8	19.2
$200,000–$500,000	58.0	29.6	28.4
$500,000–$1 million	60.5	30.4	30.1
Over $1 million	63.1	32.1	31.0

Tax Reductions Through Use of Loopholes, by Income Level

If you make	Your average yearly family income is:	The loopholes save you this much in taxes yearly
Under $3,000	$ 1,345	$ 16
$3,000–$5,000	4,016	148
$5,000–$10,000	7,484	339
$10,000–$15,000	12,342	651
$15,000–$20,000	17,202	1,181
$20,000–$25,000	22,188	1,931
$25,000–$50,000	32,015	3,897
$50,000–$100,000	65,687	11,912
$100,000–$500,000	165,998	41,840
$500,000–$1,000,000	673,040	202,751
Over $1,000,000	2,316,872	720,490

(*Money*, June 1976, p. 73). In my view, this amount is excessive and is the single largest cause of incomes seeming inadequate. Most of these taxes are assessed on a graduated scale based on total income. The equation becomes simpler when you recognize that taxes can be reduced by reducing income.

This technique, while superficially resembling financial suicide, actually makes sense. Any diversion of present income into a pension plan permits the building of a capital account that is sheltered from current taxes and that can be invested for capital appreciation. Since such deductions occur before taxes are assessed on current income, there is actually a tax saving. Part of the income that would have been paid out in taxes can be invested tax-free. Over a long period of time these savings can be compounded to provide for a more financially secure future. When you recognize that the average middle-income American is in the 25 percent tax bracket, such a savings can be substantial. Consider the following example (*Money*, June 1976, pp. 74–76):

> Consider a couple 20 years from retirement with $20,000 in taxable income, which puts them in the 32 percent federal bracket. If they put $1,500 now in a retirement fund earning 7 percent, the $1,500 will build up to $5,805 by the time they retire. If they do not put the $1,500 in a pension plan, they will lose $480 of it to taxes, leaving $1,020 to invest. The $1,020 may also earn 7 percent, but the earnings will be taxed, reducing the yield after taxes to 4.76 percent. After 20 years the couple will have $2,585—less than half what the tax-free retirement fund would produce. "Anyone who has no company pension plan and doesn't put $1,500 a year into an IRA is crazy," says tax specialist Martin Helpern of the New York office of Laventhol & Horwath, an accounting firm headquartered in Philadelphia.

We may conclude that everyone should be paying into a tax-sheltered retirement plan in order to reduce current taxes, to

The taxpayer as turnip

The Federal Income Tax Escalator
(highest rates for single taxpayers)

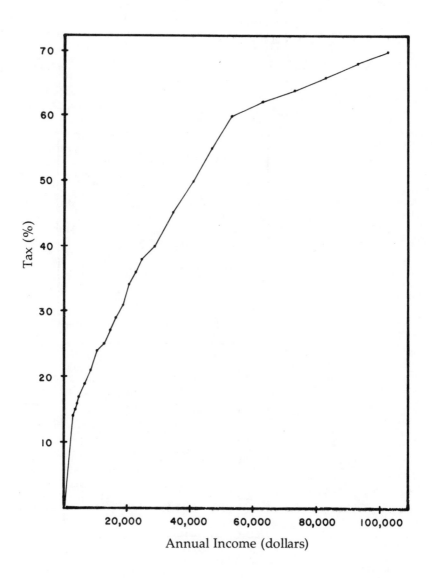

Annual Income (dollars)

build up a capital account, and to provide financial security for their future. These plans include either an employer-originated plan, an individual retirement account (IRA), or a Keogh plan. Self-employed persons, members of partnerships, and those with income from consulting, freelance writing, etc., qualify for a Keogh plan. The advantages of the latter are that you can put up to $7,500 a year into the plan, versus only $1,500 for an IRA. Company plans are good because normally your employer also contributes to the plan, but the total amount sheltered from tax is not under your control. Normally an amount equal to about 6 or 7 percent of an employee's income is invested annually under such plans. The principal advantage of all these plans is that the income on the amount invested is also free of current taxes, so your investment for the future is compounded. Of course income taxes are assessed after retirement, but normally your total income will be lower at that time; therefore the money is taxed at a lower rate. In addition, after age sixty-five there is an extra exemption that reduces the tax even further.

Alternative Views on Income Taxation

At this point it is appropriate to review the nature of the income tax and its effect on our society. The graduated scale of the tax penalizes those individuals who increase their incomes through additional efforts. Such a tax may be viewed as both a negative incentive to production and confiscatory. The steep gradient of the tax structure further leads to deliberate reductions in ceilings on income by taxpayers to avoid being pushed into a higher tax bracket. This is the reason why doctors and dentists take extended vacations, up to three months out of a year. Even turkey farmers and other self-employed individuals see no reason to augment their incomes beyond a certain point because a greater percentage must then be paid out in taxes. The actual limit that people will endure willingly seems to be at about the 20 percent level. If taxes take a higher percentage of their incomes, they become increasingly restive, and seek tax shelters or stop earning altogether. To say the least, a case can be made for reducing the top level of the graduated tax to restore incentive to the individual taxpayer.

Alternative rewards have been set up by industry for their executives simply because their salaries were being taxed out of existence. As a result, we have company-paid pension plans, direct medical benefits, housing, cars and drivers, country club memberships, deferred salary payments, stock options, hunting club privileges, etc. All of these tax-free benefits are a direct result of an unrealistically high tax on salaries above $25,000 a year.

We also have an entire field of investment stimulated as a result of these high tax levels. Municipal bonds provide tax-free income in contrast to other bonds. These tax-free bonds provide increasingly greater relief for the taxpayer in the higher brackets. Real estate with built-in depreciable assets and partnerships with tax losses that may be carried forward sell at unrealistically high prices simply because of their tax-shelter provisions. Again these provisions are of greater value to the taxpayer in the higher brackets. Another effect is speculation as a result of tax shelters. An example is the exploration for oil. Intangible drilling expenses are deductible the year in which they are incurred. Therefore someone with a tax problem can "drill up" their excess income before the end of the year. If he didn't do this, he would have had to pay the excess income out as income tax. By drilling he gets what amounts to a federal subsidy to speculate in oil discovery. If he strikes oil, he is protected by the 22.5 percent oil depletion allowance, which shelters 22.5 percent of oil income from taxation on the grounds that oil extraction depletes a nonrenewable resource. It's a good deal for the driller, but it leaves the additional tax burden for the rest of us to carry.

The next major problem is how the taxes extracted are then allocated by government. The average American knows in his heart that taxes are too high, that he has little or no control over how his taxes are spent, and that a large percentage of his taxes are wasted on ill-advised federal programs that, once begun, are never terminated. I was astonished to learn, for instance, that even though the military draft was terminated after the Vietnam War, the Selective Service Administration stayed in business. The annual budget, as I remember, was about $40 million, yet it has nothing to do!

The Cattle Baron has stated, and only partially in jest, that

154

it is your patriotic duty not to pay all of your taxes, for if you do the government will simply waste them, whereas you can better invest those funds in a productive business that will stimulate the national economy. In a way, the Cattle Baron has done just this. He owns a "widget" factory, and every time he shows a profit on his cattle he buys more widget-stamping machines and puts more people on the payroll. When widgets are selling well, he puts the excess income to work by buying more cattle or irrigation machines. The point I am trying to emphasize here is that the income-tax structure is out of control and its influence is all pervasive in the field of investments. Investments are bought and sold as tax shelters primarily, and to produce income secondarily. If you are to prosper in your investment program, it is imperative that you comprehend these tax provisions and plan your investments accordingly.

Before we leave this topic, it is appropriate to discuss cheating on one's tax return. Most people feel so harassed by taxes that they will fail to report unusual income if they believe they can get away with it. The first $100 of dividends received per year are tax exempt, but above that they are taxable. Recent studies of the income from stock dividends reveal that up to two-thirds of all taxable dividends are not declared. The situation is so bad that the IRS is contemplating a withholding program applied to dividends in order to get the millions missed every year.

The Antique Lady kept detailed records of all her individual sales. However when she had a large sale of several hundred dollars worth, she didn't report that sale at all. Her reasoning was that examination of her records would show a consistent detailed accounting that would appear to be comprehensive. Meanwhile, she had exempted a portion of her income from taxation, even though her method was illegal. (She has since sold her business and moved to a nursing home, and the statute of limitations protects her, which is why I can tell this story.)

I am sure that you know of examples of tax cheating. I am not proposing that tax cheating is acceptable behavior, I am simply stating that it is widespread and that in my opinion it is the result of a tax structure that penalizes the productive. We have a tax revolt in this country; numerous people are simply refusing to pay their taxes. One gambit is to cite the fact that

155

the Constitution specifies that only gold and silver and currency backed by them are legal tender. Those who employ this tack file a return and state that they have received no income since our currency is no longer backed by gold or silver. This principle has not been tested in court, but it seems that the IRS is not eager to have it so tested. However, it's a good bet that anyone trying this "lawful money" gambit will eventually be indicted for failure to file a correct tax return.

There is an alternative to tax cheating: restructuring your income and planning your investments in order to *legally* reduce your tax bill. I will discuss such alternatives in detail, but first let's review the effects of the tax bite on your present investment potential.

A Dollar Saved Is $1.25 Earned

Two of the principles we have already discussed are: increase your buying power through better shopping, and divert some of your present assets into equity generation rather than income production. Both practices result in greater utilization of your present income for capital appreciation rather than diluting that power through tax payments. You will increase the power of your present spending habits when you recognize that better buying achieves not only a reduction in the cost of the items purchased, but an increase in buying power (disposable income) in the amount saved *plus* the tax that would have been assessed on that amount had it been achieved as extra income. In other words, $1.00 saved is equivalent to an additional $1.25 earned. If you increase your buying power by shopping for consumer goods at garage sales, you are way ahead. At prices that you will normally find, you can buy for one dollar what usually costs five or six at retail. The average family spending $50 a month on consumer goods could buy approximately $300 worth by shopping garage sales. To be able to buy the same goods at retail, the family would have to have an increase in pretax income of $333.34 a month—$4,000 a year! Such an increase in buying power is rarely achievable any other way. No salary raise is likely to come close to this figure. The average salary raise is perhaps $500 a year, of which 25–30 percent is immediately lopped off by increased taxes. You can see why your usual raise seems so meaningless when the increased tax bite and inflation are taken into account. Obviously, internal money management provides a real tool to combat these negative influences.

Meanwhile, you can directly reduce your income-tax bill by placing a portion of your disposable income in tax shelters. Tax shelters are *not* just for the rich; they are for everybody. The most typical tax shelter is the tax-deductible interest payments on home mortgages. This provides an incentive to buy a house rather than pay rent; none of the latter is deductible. During times of inflation, the deduction of interest payments may actually provide you with a free ride on your real estate investment. If your interest rate is 8 percent and the inflation rate is 8 percent, these cancel each other out and you are paying no effective return to the mortgage holder. You are getting the use of his money free to use for your investment in real estate. Meanwhile, homeownership will protect you from additional rent increases and may even provide additional income. At the same time, you have an equity investment that may be increasing in value at a rate of 10 percent a year or more. You should consider this type of investment as one in which the interest deduction amounts to a federal subsidy to help you invest in an equity.

If you purchase income property—apartments, raw land that generates crops, etc.—then you have an even better deal. All expenses paid out to maintain the property are deductible the year they are incurred. Further, any improvements may be depreciated, which generates a further tax saving. Many apartment deals, because of their depreciation aspects, actually produce tax-free income, at least for the first five years or so. After taking that initial fast depreciation, your best bet may be to sell that property and start all over again with a new apartment package and its associated depreciation schedule. In any event, depreciation is a legal means to avoid tax on the increased income generated by your income property. On top of that, the equity in your property may also increase, so when you sell you will have had the combined benefit of a tax-sheltered income plus capital gains.

Viewed in this context, every family should acquire some

income-producing property as soon as possible. One gambit is to buy a duplex, rent half, and live in the other half. Another possibility is to move out of your house trailer into your first house and then rent the trailer. In either case you have minimized the cost of acquiring your first income property. It is therefore probably a mistake to buy the best house you can afford to live in because this ties up all of your equity and you cannot own any income property unless you refinance.

If you already live in a home you own, refinancing becomes the key to acquiring some rental property. You can figure on rental property returning an amount in excess of the costs of refinancing. Therefore, in terms of a total increase in your income, refinancing makes good sense. A further hidden saving concerns the costs spent on maintenance of a rental property. You can, for example, install new carpets in your home and move your former carpet to the rental. The old carpet represents an expense chargeable to the rental and is therefore tax deductible.

The greatest drawback to acquiring a tax shelter is that it normally requires cash on the barrel head. In addition, the sheltering aspects are usually spread out over a number of years. The net result is that you have to free up capital in advance and then wait for the savings to bring you back to your original cash position. If you don't have that initial capital, you have to become skilled at mortgage roulette in order to purchase your income property with 100 percent borrowed funds.

Winging It at 30 percent Off—the Ultimate Trip

All of the tax savings we have discussed so far, pension payments, interest payments, rental-property depreciation, and income-property maintenance, are peanuts when compared to the really big show. That really big tax shelter in the sky is yours when you go into business. Then almost anything you want becomes yours *and tax deductible*. If you are in the 30 percent tax bracket then everything you can claim as a business expense is yours at a 30 percent discount. For example, you will recall that my wife and I are in the purebred cattle business on a part-time basis, with a small herd. Even though this is less

158

than a full-time business, we can claim the full range of deductions. Here's a partial list of possible deductible items:

Livestock	Motorcycle
Pickup truck	Stationery
Camper to attend cattle events	Liquor
Airplane	Entertainment
Fencing	Recreation property
Out buildings	Meals & rooms
Travel expenses	Hardware
Cowboy clothing	Paint
Tools	Welding equipment
Gasoline & other expendable supplies	Barbeque equipment
Wiring	Office furniture & equipment
Deep freeze	A condominium if used for business purposes
Farm machinery	
Horse trailer	Anything else you can justify as a business expense

This list of deductions is pretty extensive, but could be expanded by anyone with a little imagination. For example, my wife and I both participate in cattle events as members of the breed association's promotion committee. We could both take an all-expense-paid trip to visit cattle ranches and shows in most any part of the world. Routinely, such tours are scheduled to Europe and Central America; less commonly it is possible to go to South Africa, Australia, or the Orient. At the tax-deductible rate of 30 percent off, it's not a bad deal.

We can also improve our property for recreational purposes at the same time we make a necessary ranch improvement. For example, we could construct a stock pond and at the same time stock it with trout.

You can also write off the necessary expenses for maintaining an office in your home. When you add up a percentage of the phone, electric, and heating bill, plus depreciation and maintenance on that portion of your home used for business purposes, it can help. Remember that every tax-deductible item saves you twenty-five to thirty cents on the dollar. It is normal practice to write off up to 10 percent of your housing costs for office use.

All direct business expenses are deductible in the year they occur. You need to maintain records that your dinners out were for business purposes, but that doesn't decrease the quality of the food.

Although all of these business expenses are legal where justified, the right to deduct them should be viewed as a privilege not to be abused. What is significant to you as a Penny Capitalist is that in order to enjoy any of these tax-saving blessings you have to join the system and engage in some type of business activity. The poor slob whose only income is a salary is frozen out. He is a taxpaying U.S. citizen, but his rights to fair tax treatment have been infringed by special interests. In order to exercise your rights to tax savings, you have to engage in those practices that are businesslike in nature. You can start in your basement or garage, but start *now*. Possibilities are numerous, and raising plants, sewing, or taking mail orders, can provide a means to begin charging off tax deductible expenses. Remember, some world-famous firms such as Holubar, Knott's Berry Farm, and many others began as small part-time businesses at home.

Other Shelters. Or a Leaky Roof Is Better than None

Charitable gifts can reduce your tax bite. The best kind of gift is one in which you have unrealized capital gains. An example is cited in *Money* (May 1976, pp. 76–77):

> If, for instance, you have decided to make a $500 gift and you have $500 worth of a common stock that has appreciated greatly since you acquired it, then

you should consider giving the stock rather than cash.

If you give the stock, you pay no capital-gains tax. Assume for instance, that you acquired some stock years ago for $100 and it is now worth $500. If you sell that stock, you pay tax on half the $400 gain. At a 32% tax rate, the tax on $200 is $64. By giving the stock itself, you save this amount and you still deduct $500 from your taxable income. You can buy the same amount of the same stock on the same day you make the gift, so for the cost of commissions you have your stock, a $500 deduction and no liability for tax on your $400 capital gain.

You can deduct the costs of support of your parents or other relatives. You can even donate your home to charity and live in it the rest of your life while deducting its value against current income. You can donate your collection of art objects or natural history specimens to the local museum, provided they are properly catalogued. It is also possible to set up a family trust and divert present taxable income into a financial resource for your children or grandchildren. Wealthy families have long utilized the generation-skipping tax relief provided by trusts. Today it makes sense for the not-so-wealthy to set up trusts; even a small tax-sheltered investment in effect for twenty years or more will bless your descendents with capital they could never acquire on their own.

My purpose here is not to detail every possible tax loophole; there are many references available for that. My purpose is to alert you to the fact that tax sheltering is essential to building capital. It is also a means that enables you to have your cake and eat it too. You can buy that camper or visit France for two weeks and, under the right circumstances, write off the costs as business expenses. It sounds unfair, but you should view such provisions of the tax laws as opportunities that smart people exploit and those not so smart complain about. I sympathize with those who seek to change the system to one that is more fair. Realistically, however, it seems doubtful that their efforts will bear much fruit, since every tax loophole that is closed

Idiot version of a tax loophole

costs powerful interest groups where it hurts. When their pocket-books are threatened, they will pour time and money into the fight to maintain the status quo. Pragmatically, and this is what you as a Penny Capitalist have to be, you must utilize loopholes to ease your tax burden so that you can go about your goal of building capital. You can leave the altruistic support of tax reform to those who already have their capital in hand.

Estate Planning Reduces the Tax Bite

Estate planning involves the establishment of a series of positions that govern how your assets will be available at the time you retire and after you no longer need them. Such actions, if taken now, may actually reduce your current income-tax liability and at the same time may provide funds that will be available later when you need them. The opposite tack is to let the state divvy up your estate if you die intestate (without a will).

If you are supporting your parents, you can consider establishing a reversionary trust. Income from the trust can thus be used for their support, and after their death the principal will revert to you. Meanwhile, you have reduced the demands on your take-home pay. Normally, the income your parents receive from the trust is taxed at a lower rate than it would be if you were to receive that additional income.

Even a family trust for your children's use can be helpful in the tax department. Again you divert income directly to the children for expenses that you would have to meet out of your current take-home pay. Within their standard deductions (now "zero bracket amounts"), such income will be totally free of federal income tax. Consider the advantages when such funds are spent for things you are not legally obligated to provide, such as a motorcycle or college tuition, but which you probably would cough up anyway. The trust then becomes a means to increase your real buying power through tax savings. Consider the establishment of such a trust if you have unusual income in a lump sum. You have been getting along on your present salary anyway; why not shelter that extra bonus by means of a trust? We have one for our family. It cost $500 to establish

Antediluvian estate planning

and combines our greatest indebtedness on a mortgage with our unusual outside income. The trust is permanent and provides a means to pass on to our children a portion of our estate without the liability of estate taxes. It will also generate some continuing income for our children and simultaneously reduce the income tax on our unusual outside income because of the lower taxes assessed on trust income.

Please understand that our resources aren't all that great. The fact is that every middle-income family should consider the tax-saving features of proper estate planning. After all, all wealthy people have trusts, which implies that they are financially viable enterprises. Try one yourself and see if it fits. After all, any tax-saving is a resource that I am sure you can well put to good use.

Annuities: Invest Now, Spend Later

Annuities are a new star on the horizon of the promised land as far as the middle-income taxpayer is concerned. Several aspects make these alternatives look good. In contrast to a Keogh plan, annuities can be purchased by anyone, not just the self-employed. Traditional annuities, such as those sold by insurance companies, pay ridiculously low interest rates, in the vicinity of 3 percent, and levy a sales charge as well. The new annuities are much more attractive, paying up to 7 percent, and they have built-in features that permit greater flexibility. One advantage is that income can be deferred during years of high earnings and the earnings on that income will be tax exempt during the term of the annuity, thus compounding the rate of growth. For example, under a tax-sheltered annuity, a 7 percent rate of growth compounded will quadruple your investment in twenty-one years. Under a non-tax-sheltered plan, the same return, taxed at an income tax rate of 30 percent will require an additional eight years to quadruple. Disadvantages of these annuities are that they are purchased with after-tax dollars, and they only work well if your income tax bracket is lower when you draw the funds out than when you put them in. However, it is possible to withdraw some funds at a later date tax-free, as withdrawals up to the amount originally invested are viewed as tax-exempt returns of capital.

Such annuities are primarily sold as investments by stock-brokerage firms. In addition to providing some internal flexibility in their terms, they are written in several primary forms. The deferred annuity includes a schedule of payments into the program that builds interest for a number of years, after which a schedule of repayments begins and continues for a specified term. In the event of the death of the principal, the entire amount could be passed on to his heirs subject only to the payment of estate tax. The amount received by the heirs would be exempt from income tax.

A savings annuity simply protects income derived from investments in savings certificates, certificates of deposit, and so on from income tax during the term of the annuity. The advantage is that the high rates of interest paid on such certificates can be compounded tax-free. A disadvantage is that you cannot draw out any of your invested principal prior to the maturity date of the certificates without a substantial penalty.

The investment annuity is really a tax-sheltered individual-investment account. A wide range of investments may be sheltered under one umbrella. The principal advantage is that the individual investor can manage his own assets while simultaneously achieving a tax shelter. The minimum portfolio is $10,000, but account executives prefer that portfolios under such a plan exceed $30,000, as the annual handling charges are set at one percent. Most such accounts are made up of fixed-income securities such as bonds, but common stocks may also be included. The real beauty of this gambit is that the individual investor can make his own choices instead of leaving those crucial decisions up to someone else.

The principal disadvantage of annuity plans is that in order for them to work well you have to have a reasonable sum to invest—$10,000 or more. Whereas it is possible to invest on an installment basis, this pretty much limits your participation to fixed-income securities. Another disadvantage is that, owing to the built-in feature that most gains are a result of tax-free compounding of interest, these plans are by necessity long-term and ideally fit into an estate-planning retirement account rather than a short-range capital-formation account. In addition, as always, the more you have to invest, the less are the fixed-account charges on a percentile basis. However, and this is perhaps the best feature of such plans, they form an excellent vehicle to maximize the return from an unusual or unexpected lump sum inheritance or a one-of-a-kind outside income.

Even though I have discussed these new forms of annuities in some detail, it seems fair to point out that by their design they more closely fit the needs of the conservative nonaggressive investor than they do the needs of the aggressive Penny Capitalist. They are structured to meet the needs of the middle-income investor, and that's good; such small-scale tax shelters are needed to balance the tax advantages of the really rich. Where such plans could be used in the Penny Capitalist program is in conjunction with your other capital-building schemes. When you sell something that you picked up for little or nothing, divert a portion of those gains into such a tax-free income-producing account for your retirement needs.

10

Far Out: The World of Alternative Investing

Alternative investments often afford the greatest profit potential relative to the amount of cash actually invested. By alternative investments I mean those items different from stocks, bonds, or real estate. In fact, I would exclude from that definition all securities of any type that are quoted on a daily basis by a professional brokering service, including puts, calls, options, warrants, and futures. These variants are still part of the organized securities market and as such are governed by rules and procedures established by the Securities and Exchange Commission. Further, the securities market, while presenting a fantastic variety of investment opportunities, is closely monitored by millions of investors and thousands of professional traders and brokers. As a result, the literature on the securities market is enormous and is amplified on a daily basis.

In short, investing in the securities market is a role for either the investor who is satisfied with an average return or the hard-core pros who make their living by buying and selling stocks. This is not to say that the Penny Capitalist cannot do well in the securities market, but only that it is a market dominated by full-time professionals who control enormous amounts of money in mutual funds and pension accounts. Make your initial stake first, then begin investing a portion of it in securities.

Now let's take a look at some alternative investments that make even some of the things I've discussed so far look mundane.

A Ton of Jade and Other Good Deals

About once a week the Fastest Trader in the West and I get together. We go up to a little restaurant on the hill and order a coffee and sometimes, even though we know better, a sweet roll. The conversation usually comes around to: "What have you bought or sold this week?" I am never surprised by what he has done, for the Fastest Trader in the West knows no limits in what he buys—anything that is a bargain is fair game. Nonetheless, I wasn't prepared for a ton of jade plus the slabbing saw to cut it that he picked up for a mere $2,000.

Now you may think that $2,000 for some large heavy rocks isn't that good a deal. You can't eat them, and even wearing them requires additional cutting and polishing. But the Trader's plan is to sell very small matched pieces for use as knife handles on custom-made hunting knives at $50 a pair and carved grips for revolvers at $100 and up per pair, depending upon the amount of carving. Viewed in this light, his investment seems reasonable; the saw alone is worth at least $700. I predict that he will recover his initial investment and still have most of the jade left. In the meantime, he has the prettiest rock garden in town.

About the same time, the Fastest Trader in the West made a down payment on another somewhat wild-eyed investment: a five-inch-diameter turtle carved out of agate, which will cost him about $2,000. The turtle itself isn't so valuable, even though it would appear to be of Russian craftsmanship and probably is between 100 and 150 years old. What is unique and what gives the turtle its potential for great value is that it has within it a pore space filled with water. Such trapped water sometimes occurs in agate and dates from the formation of the rock. However, such occurrences are very rare, and according to my friend, his specimen contains the largest such inclusion known. He is seeking to sell his turtle to a mineral collector for something on the order of $100,000. It sounds overly optimistic, but on the other hand, you can never raise your asking price, only lower it. His kids suggested that if the interstitial water was so valuable why not sell the water and keep the turtle!

The Trader also bought a silver-inlaid Mongolian bedpan at

a local antique shop. It was priced at about fifty dollars, as no one locally knew what it was. (Actually, it probably wasn't a bedpan either, but that description is as good as any.) He sent it to Parke Bernet in New York, where it brought $300 at auction. For all we know, the purchaser didn't know what it was either. In short, one man's bedpan may be another man's treasure.

The Cattle Baron also came up with an offbeat investment, although he can't really take too much credit because he didn't know what he was getting into. Visiting another cattle breeder, he was sitting on the porch sipping bourbon. Casually he said, "This is great bourbon." His host said, "It's bottled especially for me and I can get you some just like it." Now there is a deal for any self-respecting cattle baron—his own specially bottled drinkin' likker! The only stipulation was that the buyer had to take a full barrel in order to get in on the action. Well, the Cattle Baron put in his order because that didn't sound like too bad a deal. What he didn't realize until the truck showed up at his door was that the typical 45-gallon barrel of whiskey makes eighteen cases of twelve fifths each! His bill of $1,200 was, needless to say, somewhat more than he had bargained for. However, his price per bottle relative to the quality was a good deal.

Another deal that may seem far out to you but appeals to me is the purchase of a high-quality purebred bull. You purchase the bull, or a percentage interest, for an amount between $5,000 and $50,000. You then put the bull in a bull stud where his semen is collected. The semen is collected two or three times per week and then diluted 200 times and quick-frozen into ampules or straws. At this rate the bull can produce up to 30,000 ampules a year. The cost of collection and freezing is one dollar per ampule. You put up enough ampules to meet your needs and sell the bull. You may even sell the bull at a profit. Meanwhile, with semen selling for five to twenty dollars an ampule, you have thousands of dollars worth of semen in your tank, and it is good for at least twenty years. If the bull dies, you can write off his original cost as a tax loss, and yet you still have the useful portion of the bull in the tank.

170

Of course, you need to have either a market for the semen or a herd of your own. However the semen is valuable, and it is part of the Penny Capitalist philosophy that anything of value can sooner or later be exchanged for something else of value. It may take time and some creative thinking, but as a principle it usually holds true.

Indian crafts have been a good offbeat investment for the last decade or so. When I first learned to identify the difference between a Zia and an Acoma pot, or a Navajo blanket and a rug, twenty-five years ago, such knowledge was purely academic. For the last decade that knowledge has paid off handsomely as the market in Indian crafts boomed upward. Since 1970 the average price of baskets, rugs, pots, and jewelry has tripled or quadrupled. A lot of people didn't know which items were of good quality. Therefore you might find a Germantown yarn Navajo blanket priced at thirty-five dollars like the Fastest Trader in the West did. He traded it for enough skiing equipment to outfit his entire family. Originally that was a good deal, but unfortunately, he later spent much more than that for the metal pin in his wife's ankle after her skiing accident.

Perhaps the best Indian-craft investments are Navajo tapestries. These are small handspun, handwoven miniature rugs measuring from 15 × 20 inches to 3 × 4 feet. They are the finest Navajo weaving, with up to 120 weft threads per inch. So finely woven that they transmit light, they are premier-priced weavings selling for $1,000 to $5,000 each. These require the efforts of artists so skilled that only a handful of weavers can make them. They are rare, in fact much more rare than a Picasso painting. Therefore they are good investments even though they are expensive per square inch.

The market in such Indian crafts has peaked, and it is reasonable to expect them to increase in value at only about 10 percent a year from now on. Between 1970 and 1974 they were increasing in value at 40 percent to 100 percent per year. Part of what caused the market to spurt was the publication of an article in the *Wall Street Journal* describing what good investments they made.

On the other hand, the market in Indian jewelry is very tricky. There is so much shoddy modern jewelry with machine-stamped parts and faked-up turquoise around that the buyer should beware. In my opinion, the only way to invest in Indian jewelry today is to know the good stuff when you see it. Then you have to buy it in quantity in order to get it at a wholesale price. I bought some like this last year. It was dead pawn in a Gallup, New Mexico, grocery store—and that's a far cry from buying at Nieman Marcus or Parke Bernet!

Of course, there are bad buys in the offbeat investment market too. One of these is stamped silver ingots and commemorative plates. Initiated by a series of private mints, such offerings consist of series of medals, ingots, or plates in sterling silver. Although the metal value is there, it is usually one-fourth or less of the asking price. The mints claim these to be limited offerings that are of investment caliber. In fact, these offerings have only time limits, and numerically each series is only limited by how many can be sold. The resale market is spotty, and in my opinion, the future of these issues as investments is poor. The *Wall Street Journal* featured an article on the plates entitled "While You Were Going Under, Grannie Got In at $100, Out at $450." The impression given in the article was that "Antique Ladies" the country over had made a killing on such deals. Actually, only a few such plates experienced that kind of price rise. The majority still languish without any demonstrated resale market. Meanwhile, the mints are turning out new series hand over fist.

In my opinion, these things are worth only their bullion value. One silver "collector's plate" offered in 1973 contained silver worth $18.70 at 1973 prices. At 1978 prices the same silver would be worth about $50, a far cry from the 1973 $150 offering price of the plate. In addition, over 600,000 people have subscribed to one or more of the commemorative sets issued by the Franklin Mint alone. This represents a massive distribution to the public of items that are neither rare nor possessed of real value to match their selling price. Nothing so constituted can stand the test of time as an investment. The next move of prices on these things will be downward until a supply-demand equation is established. At that point they may become investments. If you can buy them from a disappointed investor at a price equal to their bullion value, they should make a suitable in-

172

vestment. At the prices advertised by the mints that crank them out, they are a ripoff.

A recent investment of mine was some empty oak whiskey barrels. These showed up at the local chain discount drugstore. They had about twenty of them priced at twenty dollars each. As Gertrude Stein might have said, "A good barrel is a good barrel is a good barrel." Barrels are expensive, especially when they have 110 pounds of oak apiece in them. I bought two and then asked a friend who makes wine what wine barrels are worth. His valuation of four dollars per gallon of capacity makes my barrels worth $180 each! He and I plan to make wine together. If we hadn't decided to make wine, the barrels would have been ideal to cut up and make into furniture. Planters and recreation room chairs are two projects that come to mind. I only bought two barrels, but I thought about buying all of them; I am convinced I could have advertised and sold them at forty to fifty dollars each.

Continuing our survey of far-out deals, the Fastest Trader in the West is good for another fantastic tale, about a deal that is still in progress. He began by buying an underpriced Navajo rug for $450 cash. He then traded the rug at a $1,200 valuation for an unfinished silver-mounted saddle. (Now let's face it, everyone needs an unfinished saddle, and the Fastest Trader in the West knows this, so his investment was secure.) His next step was to contact a saddlemaker, who agreed to finish the leatherwork. The Trader needed more silver conchos to make the ornamentation complete. To no one's surprise, he located a concho factory that just happened to need an engraving machine of the type he sells. So he traded the engraving machine (cost, $200) for $500 worth of conchos. His next step is to find a way to pay the saddlemaker his fee of $500. He will probably trade a gun to the saddlemaker in lieu of payment, which could leave him with a total cash investment in the saddle of $450 plus $200 for the gun. However it works out, for about $1,000 he will end up with a silver-mounted saddle that has a retail value of $10,000 to $15,000—all this in less than a year with minimal capital. We all should do as well!

How to Play the Offbeat Market

The unorganized market in offbeat items provides the greatest profit potential because you have an opportunity to pick up valuable items ahead of the general public. Investing in these offbeat items requires several techniques plus an attitudinal commitment on your part. You must become thoroughly familiar with the quality and normal price ranges of whatever you are buying. You must be able to recognize quality when you see it. For example, subtle distinctions differentiate a third-phase Navajo chief's blanket worth several thousand dollars from a twentieth-century chief's-style floor rug worth several hundred. The Antique Lady once showed me such a rug and proclaimed it to be a blanket. I was forced to tell her that it wasn't what she thought it was, but something much less valuable. A knowledge of price ranges permits you to recognize the bargain.

When you spot a bargain you have to buy it because it won't be there when you go back; someone will have snapped it up. This means that you have to develop your ability to make quick and accurate decisions. You can't go home and check your reference library; the better part of that has to be with you in your head.

Another quality that you must develop is a sense of impending market rises, recognizing what things to buy *before* a market exists for them. At such times you need to have the courage of your convictions to hang on until the rest of the world catches up with your appraisal. Once something becomes popular, a fad if you wish, you should sell it and replace it with today's bargains (tomorrow's treasures). The other side of the coin is knowing when to stop buying and sit tight. In this connection, I am no longer buying American Indian art. I am continuing to hold much of what I have to enjoy as decorator items in our home.

Between 1971 and 1975 we bought nineteenth-century pieced quilts. We actually anticipated the quilt boom by about one year. The local Quilt Man has several hundred quilts in a collection that he has been building over the past twenty years. Some of his specimens are irreplaceable, and someday they will be priceless. Our efforts in buying quilts have been much more

Victorian crazy quilt

modest. We began buying in the ten- to twenty-dollar range, and within a year prices leaped to fifty dollars. Any nondescript quilt today is priced at $75 to $100. We like the elaborate pieced and embroidered nineteenth-century quilts, but today they are almost impossible to find, so we haven't bought any quilts in over a year. Viewed as art objects the truly fine quilts are still underpriced. We bought a beauty in 1974 for $350, the most elaborate Victorian crazy quilt we have ever seen. Even though there have been many quilt shows at museums in the past several years, we have yet to see another crazy quilt as fine. We haven't sold any quilts yet, but we have given two away to friends. They make truly treasured gifts. Someday when the market is higher we may sell some.

Also in 1971 we began buying nineteenth-century oil paintings by American primitive painters. For the most part these date between 1875 and 1900. They are normally unsigned, and if they are signed, they are by artists no one ever heard of. They illustrate scenes of nineteenth-century daily life and have as much historical value as they have artistic merit. These paintings are hard to find, but are seldom priced high. In fact, we have over forty of them now, and our average cost is below ten dollars. Some day an art historian will discover this period of American art and will research it for a dissertation. When this happens, there will be museum shows, and our humble collection will dramatically increase in value.

In 1976 I began buying Mexican retablos. These are religious paintings of saints on either tin or copper. Painted in the nineteenth century, they were popular home decorations, but toward the end of the nineteenth century they were replaced by cheap colored lithographs on paper. The retablos fell into total disuse and were discarded, and for years they were both cheap and plentiful. Even as recently as ten years ago the smaller ones sold for $2.50 and the larger ones for $5.00. Today the small ones go for $15 to $30 and the larger range from $30 to $100. That's a pretty fair price jump in ten years, on the average about 700 percent to 800 percent. Taking into consideration the twenty years of price increases in other forms of art, in which multiples of several thousand percent have been recorded, retablos seem to have the potential for much additional increase in value, especially since a major study of retablo art was pub-

176

lished in 1974 and museums are beginning to feature shows of them. An art dealer I know in Mexico City tells me that retablos are now becoming hard to find, and he has switched his inventory to Mexican folk-dance masks, which he says will be next to leap upward in price. He has already sold a few large, elaborate masks with movable parts for $160 each, even though the average mask is still priced at about $10. He has 700 masks on hand waiting for the boom. I also have a few that I picked up at about five dollars each, and I'm holding them for a price rise. The Mexico City dealer also has 2,000 of the colored religious lithographs that replaced the retablos waiting for a market to develop in them.

I have been buying nineteenth-century silver ethnic jewelry as well. I began about fifteen years ago in Egypt, where handmade Nubian necklaces and bracelets were selling for their bullion value. Originally, I bought things that my wife liked and would wear. I have expanded the collection considerably over the years, and it now includes Southwestern Indian, Ethiopian, Peruvian, and Guatamalan specimens. These examples are beautiful; they have real value as art objects and in silver content; and they are about 100 years old. They are bound to increase in value. Even if we never sell them, they provide pleasure in the wearing, and they may be passed on to our future daughters-in-law. Recently, one of our close friends won a belly dancing contest, and as a symbol of recognition of her accomplishment, we gave her a North African ankle bracelet. It would have been almost impossible to find one like it on the market, and I am sure that it is one of her most prized possessions.

Over the last few years, we have also built up a collection of copper kitchen implements that my wife uses when entertaining. Our initial cost has been low because we shop the secondhand stores and buy pieces that we can refinish. The polished pieces in the antique stores sell for twenty to forty-five dollars each, whereas our average cost is about five. The secret is that we buy plated pieces (later removing the silver or nickel plate) or the lacquered pieces. Most people, dealers included, assume that lacquered copperware has a copper lacquer on some base metal. Actually, the copper lacquer is usually on top of solid copper. When a piece gets old, the lacquer chips, peels, and discolors. The result looks like a cheap product, so the item

177

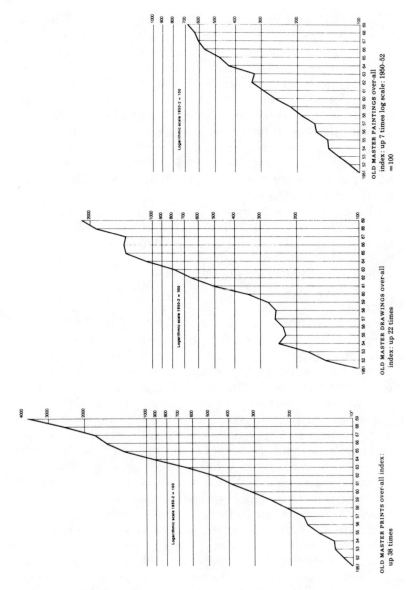

Price increases in various schools of art

178

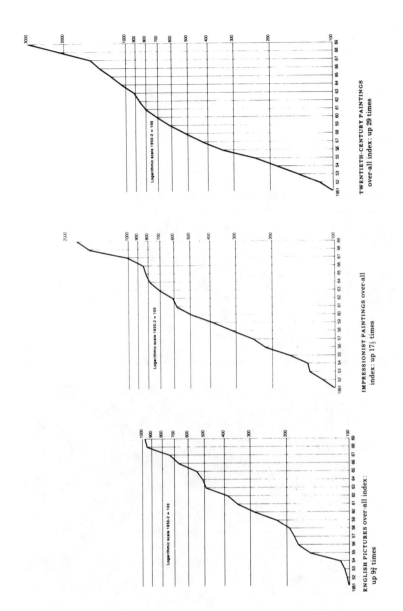

TWENTIETH-CENTURY PAINTINGS
over-all index: up 29 times

IMPRESSIONIST PAINTINGS over-all
index: up 17½ times

ENGLISH PICTURES over-all index:
up 9¾ times

179

Some recent good buys

is priced accordingly. Ten minutes work with paint remover takes off the old lacquer and reveals the solid copper underneath. Someday our daughters-in-law will be fighting over who gets that valuable collection of antique copperware!

There are lots of other items that you can pick up which will increase in value over time. A large number of these are collectible, but do not have real value. As a result, I have avoided buying such things as old comic books, Big Little Books, old movie magazines, and Avon bottles. Their scarcity is a result of limited interest over the last two decades or so. Will their value hold up for nostalgia collectors if they are reprinted or copied? If you find some, they can be sold at a profit, but I wouldn't hold them for a long-term investment.

Other items such as old bottle caps, pencils, railroad tickets, matchbook covers, playing cards, valentines, and other trivia also fall into the realm of collectibles rather than investments. They are okay to sell if you find some in an old attic, but I wouldn't pay any American dollars for them. Demand for such items is based on nostalgia or triviality, and such a demand is properly considered a fad. Thus these things may not be termed investments. I would also include in this same class dolls, powerline insulators, barbed wire, mason jars, buttons, and souvenir spoons, although I know there are those who would disagree with me.

The Fastest Trader in the West told me about another gambit he has used to increase his equity. He showed me an Indian peace medal of bronze. Today these medals are priced at $100 or better on the antique market. What most people don't know is that these medals can still be purchased new from the Smithsonian Institution at about seven dollars each! I am sure you could trade any of these medals at a local gun show for $100 worth of old guns, knives, spurs, etc.

The Organized Market in Collectibles

The organized market in collectible items provides a network of dealers, magazines, and newspapers that disseminate information and prices. In addition, there are regularly updated

181

price guides that list items by type, quality, and price. This type of market is difficult to make money in because (1) the dealers are totally informed and, (2) the only way to buy wholesale is to buy in large quantities. Normally the opportunities (if you may call them that) for the individual investor are to buy at retail from a dealer and then sell at wholesale back to a dealer when the market has moved up. This is not really investing, but is more on the order of financial suicide.

For example, the stamp market is one in which I have dabbled. I converted some blocked Egyptian currency by buying a collection of good-quality British colony stamps in Cairo. Back in the States I put them up at auction. Each day collectors would sort through the stamp albums and note their bids on individual stamps. Once a month those stamps bid on would be termed sold. The dealer took a 20 percent commission and I got the rest. At this rate it took me about six months to get my money back. It was a nit-picking, niggarly investment that wasn't worth the time and effort involved. I still have the remainder of the unsold stamps, but they are not among my prized investments. While in Egypt I could also have bought sheets of unused U.S. commemorative stamps. These bombs— which boobs still line up to buy at every new issue—resell at *less* than face value. The investment potential in U.S. commemoratives is simply to buy them as cheaply as possible and then use them up as postage. Here again you can save some money, but it is no big deal. The real biggies in stamp investment buy known rarities as hedges against inflation. They are okay for that purpose, but other items like paintings or other art objects can serve the same function and are more decorative to own. Again, you have to pay a commission in order to sell.

Another stamp investment is buying mint-condition singles or issues or even multiple sets of issues. There is an active market in such sets, but their price depends upon their rarity. In order to achieve a gain you have to learn which issues are underpriced relative to their rarity, then wait for the market to catch up with you. This is too risky for the Penny Capitalist because it requires specialized knowledge comparable to that needed for currency speculation. In case this gambit turns you on, however, you can start by consulting Edward J. Zegarowicz' *Inflation-Proof Your Future*. Zegarowicz explains this kind of investing in great detail and gives advice on investing in coins, autographs, rare books, etc. His book is so good that I have seen it plagiarized. I won't do that here, but will simply give my opinion on the appropriateness of these investments for the Penny Capitalist.

To return to stamps as an investment, my experience has been most negative. I joined a stamp club once and went to meetings. Everyone had boxes full of duplicates that no one else wanted—not even in trade. One collector had a lifetime investment in early U.S. issues in mint condition. He was trying to sell them at 50 percent of catalog value—with no takers. These were prize items, and yet the market was too thin for him to move them easily. Neophytes seldom understand the relationship between catalogue prices and the real stamp market. Dealers try to sell at 40 to 50 percent of catalog value and buy at 10 to 20 percent. Frankly, I think the whole stamp thing is overrated as an investment, and it is best left to little old men in green eyeshades and house slippers.

In recent years there has been a tremendous flurry of activity in coins, bags of circulated silver coins, single gold coins in common issues (if their mint dates differ from their date of issue, they are called bullion coins), uncirculated coins in rolls, and single coins of numismatic interest. All of these have boomed upward in price, especially in the last ten years, as silver coins have been replaced with those of nickel, copper, and aluminum. Gold coins have been at a premium as hedges against inflation and deflation as well.

Where will the market stabilize, and which of these alternatives are in fact investments? Several facts are relevant. I have seldom found coins at a bargain anywhere in the world. I have seen them offered in coin shops, flea markets, antique shops, jewelry stores, and market stalls in Europe, Africa, and South and Central America, as well as the U.S. Normally they are overpriced relative to their condition. Further, they are priced at retail as listed in some catalog. Even the little old peasant woman selling in the street market wants the world retail price. Frequently the coins are mutilated or badly worn, and the price is that quoted for coins in good condition. In short, there are no bargains! Some of these coins I buy for use in jewelry if they are ancient, like pieces of eight. I bought some of these in Peru, and out of curiosity, asked a local coin dealer what they were worth. His offering price was less than I paid for them, and I bought from one of those little old Inca ladies in peasant costume!

The organized coin shops push the buying of uncirculated rolls of U.S. coins as investments. These stunners are backed by impressive records of past increases in value. Part of this increase is due to the fivefold increase in silver prices in the past decade. The rest of the increase is due to increased demand by investors. In other words, this market is highly inflated by the very people who claim that they are investing for the long pull. Prices may well increase in the future, but the present price levels seem to me to be unrealistic. In fact, the entire market in uncirculated rolls is based on a kind of chainletter approach. Profits are made by those in first unloading to those in last. The coins in rolls are not rare; in fact, in most cases millions are in existence. As an investment these rolls appear to me to be highly questionable. On the other hand, a man in my home town was putting everything he had into uncirculated rolls in the 1950s and early 1960s. He got in ahead of the crowd and is worth a bundle today. Your chances of buying in today and repeating his record are pretty slim. Besides, you have to pay a commission to sell.

Bags of circulated silver bullion, or "junk," coins are different. They are sold in face-value lots of $1,000 per bag. The price of these coins fluctuates in relationship to the silver market. Since silver is widely used in industry and is being used faster than it is being produced, these coins seem to be an excellent hedge against inflation as well as an excellent investment for the long pull. In addition, since the coins are legal tender, they have a bottom-side value (their face value) in case of a major depression. In the event of a depression you could use these coins to pick up other equities at bargain prices. A final advantage of junk silver coins is that they are rapidly being used up by jewelry craftsmen. Therefore, even though they are of common dates and circulated condition, they are becoming scarcer through attrition, and thus worth more.

Numismatic coins are tremendously inflated. Their prices bear no relationship to their intrinsic metallic value. When the gap between price and metallic value ranges between three hundred and several thousand percent, the downside risk seems excessive. While numismatic coins are touted as hedges against inflation, they are already badly inflated themselves. Further, they may easily be faked by centrifugal casting; most of the "U.S. gold coins" that I have seen for sale in foreign countries were highly suspect. In short, investing in numismatic coins requires both considerable capital and knowledge. It doesn't seem to me to meet to the needs of the Penny Capitalist, at least not when you buy from a dealer.

The purchase of numismatic coins at auction is another kind of opportunity. One aspect of the coin market is that collectors are most common in the country of origin, so at auction the bargains are foreign coins. At one auction I attended in Canada, the Canadian silver dollars went sky high. The Mexican pesos at the same auction were dirt cheap. Buying at auctions, you can get foreign coins and then reconsign them in their country of origin for a possible profit.

The so-called gold bullion coins were minted in large quantities and are neither rare nor, strictly speaking, numismatic coins, having been minted over long periods of time with the same mint date. Nonetheless, they are the perfect double hedge against inflation and deflation. Their bullion content is known, and therefore, they can be exchanged without any need for assay. Furthermore, gold is the ultimate world standard of value. Nothing else in human history is equivalent to gold as a store of value. When the peasant women of the world begin wearing paper money around their necks, then and only then can you feel safe in exchanging gold for some government's printed paper. As Ludwig von Mises said, paper is the only commodity of value that government can slap ink on and make totally worthless!

Rare books are another opportunity. Factors that determine the value of a book are scarcity, condition, edition, overall quality, and the fame of the author. In general, books on specific nonfiction subjects retain their value better than works of fiction. The book market is highly specialized and requires much knowledge. Most books of any real value were expensive when they were printed and therefore were issued in a limited quantity. If you inherit a collection, have it appraised before selling.

185

However, your chances of picking up real values cheaply in secondhand shops aren't very good. I have bought a few, but only in subjects I was interested in, and I plan to keep them for my own use. Here again, buying rare books as a hedge against inflation and for investment normally requires buying from a dealer, buying at retail and later selling at wholesale. To get underpriced bargains you have to know more than the dealer.

Autographs are a real sleeper. Most people never consider that signed old documents have any real value. The expensive ones are significant documents signed by important people. To have a document or simply an autograph signed by a famous person may not suffice because lots of movie stars and other personalities sign autographs and photos and distribute them like confetti. What are most valuable are documents signed by U.S. presidents and other important officials. There is an auction market, so if you find something in your aunt's attic, you can sell it. I picked up three documents at a garage sale for fifty cents each. One is dated 1878 and is signed by the secretary of the treasury. Another dated 1900 is signed by a U.S. senator. The third is a mortgage made out to Seneca Howland. He is famous for going part way down the Colorado River with John Wesley Powell. Howland changed his mind and started to return overland with a partner. Both were killed by Ute Indians. Now, with a story like that to go with an old piece of paper, wouldn't you feel the document had some value?

Paintings and Prints

Works of art make outstanding investments because they are beautiful and can be used to improve the quality of your home. Meanwhile, they appreciate in value. Even if you never sell them, you always have that possibility, so owning art is analogous to having a nest egg in the bank. Further, you may have the opportunity to donate some art to your local museum for a tax deduction. A final consideration is that art is very nice to pass on to the younger members of your family, either as gifts or as part of your estate. Investing in art can be a short-term

186

affair, but more often it is for the long haul, and in the meantime, you are enriching your life and the lives of those around you.

Most people are afraid to invest in art because they believe it to be so esoteric they can't understand it. If you feel this way, you should buy something that you like and then learn everything that you can about it. There are large numbers of books in any public library on every aspect of art. Check them out and study both the text and illustrations. Before long, you will be confident that you can tell one type from another. Go to the local art museum and study those examples you like.

Meanwhile, you should also study the Sotheby–Parke Bernet catalogs and learn something about prices.* Art prices are often unrealistic, so you must carry your own appraisal mechanism with you in your head. When investing in art I strongly recommend that you buy only those things you like. Then if you make a poor purchase in an investment sense, at least you won't be saddled with something you can't bear to look at.

One day, while going to coffee with the Fastest Trader in the West and the Basket Man, I remarked that I was going to learn about paintings and would begin buying them as investments even though at that time I didn't know anything about them. My only purpose in mentioning this here is that all it really takes to become knowledgeable in the art market is the determination to set that goal and then follow through with study. Since then I have bought Spanish colonial paintings, retablos, a Catlin lithograph, and some American primitives, to go with the two Greek Orthodox icons and several paintings done by a contemporary friend that I already had. I also like American Western art, the Taos School, and the nineteenth century Hudson River School, but so far haven't found the funds to get into those markets.

Art dealers are a snobbish lot and try to impress the shopper with a sales pitch larded with jargon. For the most part, I ignore what they say, as in most cases they are trying to sell paintings on the basis of endorsements that have little to do with the

---

* These catalogs are available in your local library or by mail from Sotheby–Parke Bernet, 980 Madison Ave., New York, NY 10021.

quality of the work. Good art has a magic to it, and you can train your eye to recognize that magic even under layers of dirt and old varnish. If you can't see the quality, it probably isn't there, no matter what the dealer says. Most contemporary art is worthless no matter how high it is priced, but there are two aspects of contemporary art that bear special mention. The modern schools are quite faddish—therefore, whatever is popular today and selling at several thousand dollars a painting may well be worthless tomorrow.

In addition, the commercialization of contemporary art follows a prescribed pattern. Dealers carry certain artists on contract. The dealers schedule shows and push the works of those artists in their stables. The artists, if popular, become recognized for their style. Their popularity requires that to meet the demand they must paint works that are clearly recognizable as theirs. This system stifles creativity, and the very quality of art that is precious is sacrificed to meet the demands of the marketplace. All you have to do is visit the galleries on Fifty-seventh Street in New York to see this practice in action and to recognize its sterility.

If you want to invest in art, I recommend that you take a course in art appreciation simply to become familiar with the major schools and types of art available. Then choose an art form that you like and study it intensely. Eventually, you will build your knowledge to the point where you are ready to buy. Part of your knowledge should include the kind of market history summarized in Richard Rush's *Art as an Investment* (1961). After all, as a potential investor you need to know whether your area of interest has increased in value by a factor of six or forty in the past twenty years. The future price potential should depend in part on the recent price history.

Buying art is a specialized activity, and you need to know the details of the trade. I will not cover these here because there are numerous other comprehensive works on the subject. Briefly, the value of paintings is influenced by the popularity of the school, recognition of the specific artist, the quality, and the availability of similar works on the market. Attribution is critical. A work may either be signed by the artist and known to be his work, or be attributed to his studio (which means

188

parts were done by his apprentices). Or it may simply be claimed to be in his style, or a verified copy of his work. There is no market for copies of important paintings. All of these distinctions are indicated in auction catalogs by a delicate gentleman's code. You have to learn this code in order to buy art at auction with confidence.

A further consideration is the price appreciation that occurs after the death of an artist. Often this is the direct result of promotion. For example, the Art Dealer acquires estate collections of deceased artists. Once he has a sizable portion of the available work of that artist corralled, he schedules a show of that artist's work and commissions a retrospective catalog of the artist's life work. The ensuing publicity makes that artist's canvases boom upward in price, and guess who just happens to have them for sale? It is good business, but it can also benefit you if you have researched your topic and bought similar paintings before the boom.

I have to digress here to tell you a bit about the Art Dealer, one of my favorite characters. He bought 20,000 strands of African trade beads and parleyed those into his art gallery. Somewhere along the way he also bought and resold at a profit a truckload of cowboy hats. Now that he is respectable, he has a staff of eleven people, a $500,000 line of credit at the bank, and an inventory worth $7 million. He did all this in about five years by promoting a school of art that previously was selling at one-fifth to one-tenth of its current value.

To recap, some of the basic art investment rules outlined above include:

- Learn about art first.

- Buy something you like.

- Don't let the dealers dazzle you with jargon.

- Learn the jargon yourself.

- Specialize in the lower-priced schools and artists.

- Plan to buy for the long term.

189

Another aspect we must discuss is condition. Most paintings of any value are old, and some are very old. Age causes deterioration, and periodically, paintings must be cleaned or, if damaged, restored. There is a great mystique about restoration of paintings, and most conservationists are very secretive about their techniques. Most of this secretiveness is unwarranted. What the pros are afraid of is that people with no training will ruin a painting by using a commercial paint remover.

In fact, the restoration of paintings is not all that mysterious, but it does combine knowledge with skill. Since every painting *may* require a unique combination of solvents plus use of physical techniques, cookbook-type recipes will not work. The restorer must use his critical judgment step by step. However, it is possible to work wonders with a damaged painting if you know how. While studying at the provincial museum in Victoria, Canada, I worked on paintings under the supervision of the museum's painting conservator. I bought old junk paintings in terrible shape in an effort to find something that was beyond hope. Every painting taught me more, and I learned that if the intrinsic value is great enough hardly any painting is beyond saving. Often the paintings that looked the worst were actually intact beneath a discolored varnish layer.

Even if you never attempt restoration yourself, you should learn about its limits because the best bargains for the Penny Capitalist are those paintings that superficially look in poor shape. Such knowledge helps in your appraisal of any paintings you may seek to buy. It makes it possible for you to identify important aspects that directly affect the authenticity and value of a painting. For example, imagine my surprise when visiting a major art museum in this country on realizing that their entire gallery of French Impressionist paintings were painted on *new* canvases! These were supposedly works of such artists as Van Gogh and Gauguin, and would therefore have to have been a minimum of seventy years old. The collection had been given to the museum by a famous oil man–politician for a tax write-off. I think you can figure out the rest of the story.

Another category of art investment is prints. Prints are popular to collect because they are relatively inexpensive and plentiful. I never buy prints, because of those reasons and because modern reproduction methods make it extremely difficult to distinguish between an original print manufactured and signed by the artist and a photoengraved copy that is worthless. My preference is to buy only oil paintings because I can recognize them, whereas prints provide too many opportunities to be fooled. Further, it is possible to buy an authentic painting of a school that is out of vogue for less than many prints of artists and schools that are in vogue.

In sum, my advice on buying art as an investment is to buy quality in what you like and wait for the market to catch up with you.

Fakes and Reproductions

Fakes are items deliberately manufactured to be sold as the real thing, while reproductions are made to provide a substitute for the real thing at a low price. Unfortunately, these two classes tend to become indistinguishable after a reproduction is sold by its initial owner. A general rule is that most fakes and reproductions can be distinguished from the original by careful study. The wary buyer must be able to do this, and the primary way to do so is to examine closely details of workmanship and materials.

Even experts are sometimes fooled, and when this happens, in some ways it doesn't matter. If the fake is that good, the artistic quality *is* there! For example, there are the famous paintings by Van Meegeren, which he signed "Vermeer," and the sculptures in the classical style by the twentieth century Italian, Dossena. Recently I was told of a multi-thousand-dollar purchase of a Mesoamerican Pre-Columbian pot by the director of a national museum. The conservation staff of that same museum examined the paint and determined that it contained white lead, which was not used prior to 1920!

A further general rule is that the more expensive the item, the more likely it is a fake. Today the market is flooded with reproductions of nineteenth century art glass, ancient Greek and Roman coins, U.S. gold coins, French impressionist paintings, Pre-Columbian pottery, etc. There are even baskets made of raffia in the style of the California mission Indians. These are not properly either fakes or reproductions, as they were

My modern fake of a nineteenth century New Mexico reliquary

made in the 1920s by little old ladies in basketry classes. However, the unwary believe them to be authentic American Indian baskets. There are also Navajo-style rugs made in Mexico on mechanical looms. You may rest assured that sooner or later you will buy a fake. When you do, resell it, someone else will probably pay about what you did.

Just for fun I made a nineteenth century New Mexican–style reliquary for a retablo. I used old lumber and new square nails, which I rusted with nitric acid. I gave it to the Fastest Trader in the West and he thinks it's a great joke to fool people with. You would be surprised what one can do with old lumber, old leather, and rusty iron. Bear this in mind the next time you shop at a flea market or auction.

Old Cars

Automobiles as investments may seem far out to some and totally incomprehensible to others. After all, the average family automobile is burdened with an extremely rapid depreciation rate, which constitutes a consumer expense rather than an investment. But it's a different story with antique and classic automobiles; they appreciate in value. Recently in California a 1929 Mercedes SSK sold at auction for $150,000. Other unique automobiles, such as Hitler's limousine, the Bonnie and Clyde death car, and cars built especially for royalty, command prices nearly as high. In my home town there is an unusual kind of car lot. Vintage American cars of the 1940s and '50s are offered for sale at prices of $1,000 or so. Many of these need a total rebuilding to be made serviceable.

What exists, then, is a hobby and collectors' market for old cars. Those examples that are rare or beautiful or both find a ready market. There are regular auctions, newspapers, magazines, and even swap meets that cater to the old-car collector. At the swap meets you can find that fender or radiator ornament you need, as well as buyers for your surplus treasures.

I have researched the market to some degree and can report that automobiles depreciate for about ten years. At that point those cars of collector interest begin to appreciate again. Meanwhile, ten-year-old cars of no collector interest continue depre-

193

In those days, there was only one thing to do with money: Save it.

Well, the Son did exactly as his Father had advised and put the $5000 in a bank! Then, 40 years later, on HIS Son's 18th birthday:

Well, the Son obeyed his Father's wishes and put the $13,000 in the bank. Then, 26 years later, the Son told the story to HIS Son and gave him the money, now grown to $20,000...

Here, Son, and there's a lesson in **thrift** you can learn from that original $5000! Do you know what $20,000 can **buy** today?

But if your Grandpa had **bought** a Stutz Bearcat instead of putting that $5000 in the bank, what would **you** have **now** . . .?

One thing I can't stand is a smart- ass kid!!

Yeah! About what **$5000** could buy **65 years ago!**

An antique automobile worth about **$45,000!!**

ciating down to zero. For investment purposes your best buys at the moment are ten-year-old sports cars such as the Jaguar XKE, Mercedes sports coupe, and the Alfa Romeo. Cars of real luxury such as the Rolls Royce, Bentley, and Mercedes 600 limosine are also good buys in their middle age. Even if they do not appreciate dramatically as you hold them, they hold their value and provide real service with a flair.

A unique occurrence of the last few years is that some recent-model cars have actually increased in value across the board. The most outstanding examples are the late-model Mercedes. For example, a 1968 model sold for less money on the resale market in 1973 than the same car does today. Meanwhile, the lucky owner of the car has driven it cost-free. One of my friends has had three late-model Mercedes in the 1970s. He states that the increase in their value has offset all of his operating expenses.

Buying a used Mercedes is an interesting experience in itself. I have recently done this, so this discussion is not just academic. Imagine my surprise to learn that used Mercedes are priced on dealers' lots at $1,500 to $2,000 above the book retail value. What this means is that the Mercedes dealers are giving super-high trade-ins in order to move their new automobiles. If you get into this game with cash, your first purchase is at an outrageously high level. However, once you are on the inside, a Mercedes owner, you can trade up and maintain most of your equity in your present car. It is an interesting contrast to the American car situation. In the Mercedes market you buy high and stay high. In the American car you buy cheaper and depreciate out to zero over a short term.

We bought a diesel, which reduces our operating costs. There are no tune-up costs and diesel fuel is much cheaper than gasoline. We get twice the mileage, and fuel costs about 20 percent less per gallon. Altogether, we have cut our fuel costs by 50 percent to 60 percent as compared to a gasoline-powered car. Further, we are hedging against future increases in gasoline costs.

At this point I must tell you about our experience investing in old cars, not because it was a great investment but because it is a great story. My son, at that time eleven years old, was a great car buff. He could identify every make and model and tell you their performance characteristics. He had had a collection of tiny car models since he was five, and avidly read *Road and Track, Car and Driver*, and other such children's literature. After raising a calf on a bottle for his initial grubstake, he informed me that he was going to buy a sports car. I felt the best way to cope with his mania was to tell him to go ahead, since I doubted he could achieve his goal with his fifty bucks. He called up car dealers, visited their lots, and even knocked at the doors of houses when he spotted old sports cars littering their driveways. The times I was with him I felt compelled to inform people that he wasn't really a midget but simply an eleven-year-old who knew a lot about cars.

He finally located a 1963 Sunbeam Alpine, for which he offered sixty dollars. The seller rather kindly offered to take fifty. The car would actually run, although it needed an engine overhaul and the body was a cancer victim. To solve this problem we visited salvage yards and came up with a 1962 Sunbeam with an excellent body but a motor in pieces. I still don't know where my son got the money to pay for that one. Towing that car home was a nightmare because we lost a wheel in heavy traffic on the freeway. Suffice it to say that we finally accomplished our mission.

We next contacted an auto mechanic friend who agreed to combine our cripples and make one car out of two. Accordingly, we hauled the parts up to his cabin in the mountains. Six months later we had to dig the car parts out of a snowbank; our "friend" had left town unexpectedly, the victim of nonemployment and other ills.

Our next effort was to have the engine rebuilt at an auto repair shop operated by our rental tenant. Surely this would work out. Well, six months went by and all we got were excuses why the parts hadn't been delivered. We found out later that the parts had never been ordered because the man didn't have the seventy dollars needed to buy them. Meanwhile, he didn't pay his bills—including the rent for his shop. The next time we heard anything, our car parts had been sold by the shop-building owner in a bankruptcy sale!

We contacted the buyer, who agreed to work things out. He would rebuild the engine for $500. We agreed to his proposition. This time the promises came true. The engine was rebuilt and would even run. Unfortunately, the total bill came to $893. We paid up, believing that we would recoup our losses in gasoline savings.

How naïve we were not to realize that gasoline savings are proportionate to miles driven. We couldn't keep the Sunbeam running for more than a week at a time. So between trips to the car hospital, and days and weeks spent with the thing sitting dead in its tracks in our driveway, we were able to put about 1,000 miles on the car over a six-month period.

At this point we decided to sell and take our loss like men. We advertised to no avail. At the same time my oldest son had found a car he wanted to buy, a 1972 Volvo in good running condition. The Volvo owner agreed to consider the Sunbeam in trade. By this time the Sunbeam wouldn't start because its starter had died. We quickly attached a chain and were able to pull start it. When the Volvo owner arrived, the Sunbeam was running smoothly. He agreed to give us a $600 trade-in, and we were off the hook, although some $500 had gone down the tubes in the process. Every once in a while we see the Sunbeam advertised for sale in the local paper, and we once saw it sporting a For Sale sign.

The moral to this long and involved story is that old cars can be an investment if you have the capability to do your own repairs. Also, it should be noted that some auto mechanics are the least trustworthy element of our society residing outside of jail.

My son is now into motorcycles.

Goodies Away from Home Plate

Few investors seem to realize that some of their best opportunities for low-cost investments occur in foreign countries. The typical pattern is that the investor puts all of his eggs in his investment basket at home. When he does travel to other countries his attitude is simply that of a tourist on vacation and he limits his purchases to cheap souvenirs like carved gourds or brightly colored seed beads.

This is simply an ostrich-in-the-sand approach. I have already pointed out that the time to pick up a bargain is when you see one. Frequently in the markets in foreign countries, real bargains exist. The best example I can remember turned up while I was shopping in Egypt after the Nasser revolution. The wealthy had been forced to leave the country, leaving most of their possessions behind. The antique shops were full of paintings, European art glass, etc. I could have bought several vases of cameo glass signed by Emile Gallé for ten dollars each. They were small and could have easily fitted into a suitcase. Not recognizing their value, I didn't buy any; in fact, at that time I didn't even know what they were. Imagine my surprise to learn after returning to the U.S. that they were worth ten times the Egyptian asking price.

Since then I have followed a more consistent pattern of attempting to pick up enough bargains on a foreign trip to equal my expenses. The net result is an expenditure of funds, but at the same time the establishment of an equal amount of new equity holdings. Viewed as a long-range plan, the ultimate net result is that eventually the foreign travel will have been made free. By following this plan in various countries, I have so far bought silver jewelry, paintings, art glass, coins, stamps, handwoven clothing, and books. Similarly, my brother bought some antique peasant costumes embroidered with silver wire. These are true museum quality specimens and are beautiful to behold.

Even when you do not invest in items for eventual resale you may be able to bring back items that cut your cost of living at home. I think of the beautiful hand-woven shirts and jackets that I bought in the market at Chichicastenango, Guatemala. They sell for twenty-five to seventy-five dollars apiece here, but cost only five to ten there. I have already mentioned my chance to buy U.S. commemorative stamps at discount in Egypt. There are lots of opportunities, and they range from gold ethnic jewelry to uncut gemstones and other items of real value to primitive art and European manufactured antique guns and watches.

The principle you have to employ in this gambit is to think small: The items have to fit into your suitcase. The other aspect of such ventures is that you have to clear U.S. customs coming back. Therefore you must either spend less than $100 for items of recent manufacture or pay duty. Original works of art and items that are over 100 years old are duty-free. Shop in the right categories and you should have little trouble with customs. I did have trouble once when a customs man refused to believe the Cowichan sweaters I bought in a Canadian thrift shop were actually used. My cost was only about 20 percent of their value, and he found that equally hard to believe.

As you know there is another market for items purchased abroad, namely, marijuana, heroin, etc. I don't need to discuss in detail how this type of purchase does not fit your investment plan! What you may not realize, however, is that the U.S. Fish and Wildlife Service people are real bloodhounds when it comes to tracking down imported products derived from animals on the endangered species list. Therefore turtle shells, whale teeth, walrus tusks, and other goodies are no-nos. Other items may transmit diseases, such as parrot fever from feathers. There is a lively market for all these items because they are used in American Indian arts and crafts and in Indian ceremonial costumes. As an unplanned example of what can happen, though, we bought a stuffed hawksbill turtle in Mexico in 1972 at a cost of four dollars for our son's collection of natural history specimens. Since then that turtle species has been placed on the endangered list, and the turtle shell today is priced at thirty-five dollars a pound. We have a successful investment if we should ever decide to sell our legally obtained turtle.

Another example of a foreign derived specimen is even wilder. We attended a local charity auction only to be presented with the opportunity to buy a mounted action group consisting of a mongoose attacking a cobra. I believe it was imported from Taiwan for resale here. In any event, my sons were determined that we should buy it, so I bid it in at six dollars. It wasn't much of a buy at that because our youngest son began having nightmares about snakes. So we reconsigned it to another auction and sold it for twenty-five dollars. At that we didn't get top dollar; similar specimens were priced at $160 at the local airport shop. The conclusion to be emphasized here is that you should be alert for foreign bargains. They may well reimburse you for much of the cost of your travel, even when your trip is only to a local auction.

Other forms of foreign investment include stocks and bonds, income accounts, and land. All of these may be good investments, although they are subject to regulation by non-U.S. laws, which are often restrictive. Nonetheless, numerous investors have made out well having their funds in foreign bank accounts paying 10 to 14 percent. Such investments, and this includes land, provide a hedge against excessive taxation or inflation at home and provide a measure of safety through diversification. Some people I know have foreign bank accounts and enjoy the proceeds thereof on annual vacations to their foreign base of operations. One thing that is not fully appreciated is that many small nations have a shortage of capital and reward foreign investments with high interest rates. In addition, some foreign nations are not too concerned about U.S income tax laws and do not report the income paid on their foreign accounts. In fact there are numerous foreign-based tax-exempt investment opportunities. Some basic research in this area of investments could pay off handsomely. However, a basic rule of thumb is that you need to go to the country in question and learn something about its business and political practices before you take the big plunge with your hard-earned or hard-borrowed dollars.

Land is an especially good investment because it can provide a low-cost retirement haven. We own land in Canada and have investigated similar opportunities in Mexico. Such opportunities do not include subdivisions promoted by your local real estate agent. If you receive a brochure in the mail promoting a beach resort somewhere with a toll free number to call—forget it. Such deals, with their expense-free inspection trips, are so far from the ground floor that you need a space capsule for reentry to the Penny Capitalist's world.

Comments on the Organized Securities Market

In contrast to the offbeat market in collectibles, buying and selling on the stock market is the investment medium that is proclaimed by most investment counselors as the best for most small investors. Their reasons include the daily availability of prices quoted, volume, short sales, odd lot sales, and other market indicators. The idea is that this wealth of information provides a degree of safety not available in other forms of investment. They cite the ease of buying and selling as another endorsement: You can buy or sell any day of the week by means of a phone call. They further endorse the wide variety of opportunities ranging from options to stocks, bonds, and mutual funds. In their view this plethora of investment opportunities meets the needs of every investor in an individual manner. In other words, if your investment interests include safety of principal and yield, or growth, or leverage, or any other goal, you can do it all in the market.

I disagree with this, not in principle, but in practice. While the market provides such opportunities, it is also infinitely confusing in its complexities. Further, it is infested with professionals who spend their entire waking lives figuring out ways to wedge out a small fortune. We have an endless chain of insiders extending from corporation executives to floor traders, brokers, investment counselors, mutual fund managers, the market letter publishers, and mutual fund salesmen. It is my contention that the net result of this chain of insiders is a network of information that is both baffling and structured to deceive. I pointed out earlier how the public was gulled into buying Occidental Petroleum all the way down during its monumental selloff, while the insiders were getting out. I contend that the Penny Capitalist should have some funds invested in the market as an educational device. However, he should have modest goals taking into account the secondhand and biased nature of all the information he has access to. He needs this educational training in order to later invest for a moderate return after he has accumulated his basic capital through other investments.

For example, sample portfolios were presented in the April 1974 *Money* magazine for four couples at four stages in life, one in their twenties, one in their thirties, one in middle age, and one nearing retirement. Had you followed this advice, invested accordingly, and then held until March 1978 to sell, the *loss* of your original capital would have been as follows, exclusive of commissions and taxes:

Twenties	45%
Thirties	2
Middle Age	28
Nearing Retirement	13

If we adjust for the loss of 25 percent in buying power caused by inflation over the past four years, the investors' remnant buying power looks like this:

Twenties	41.25%
Thirties	73.50
Middle Age	54.00
Nearing Retirement	65.25

In summary, the recommended portfolios weren't so hot for those seeking either to accumulate capital or generate income while maintaining the buying power of their nest egg.

11

OPM:What You Can Get Free

OPM stands for "other people's money," and whenever you can do it, it's better to spend theirs instead of yours. I am here referring to expense accounts, grants, and cost sharing. All of these possibilities provide the opportunity to meet some of your expenses with funds provided by others. The unique aspect of most of these deals is that they are tax-free. Every dollar of OPM is worth $1.25 in pretax earnings. It is to your advantage to find out how much of this "free" money you can pick up.

The easiest funds to acquire are those for travel, rooms, and meals. Commonly your employer will spring for these when it is directly in the company's interest for you to travel. It is even possible to convince your employer that such travel is to his advantage when he may not have thought of it on his own. After all, such expenses represent a tax-deductible operating expense to your employer, and if it is for a worthwhile cause, he may well approve your request.

Over the years I have engaged in such travel for professional purposes, and the list below gives some indication of the sources I have tapped.

National Science Foundation
Wenner Gren Foundation
Smithsonian Institution
Rockefeller Foundation
National Institutes of Health
U.S. Forest Service

American Philosophical Society
Ft. Burgwin Research Center
Southern Methodist University
Texas Tech Museum

Crown Zellerbach Corp.
El Paso Natural Gas Co.
Colorado School of Mines
Museum of New Mexico
Instituto de Antropologia de Honduras
Instituto de Antropologia y Historia de Mexico
Province of Alberta

Canadian Research Council
Egyptian Geological Survey
Bella Bella Indian Tribe
National Park Service
B. C. Packers Corp.
Banco Central de Nicaragua
University of Calgary
Banco Centroamericano

So far, these organizations have enabled me to take one trip around the world, three trips to Europe, four to Central America, one to South America, and one to East Africa. The majority of expenses have not been paid by myself, and the trips have ranged from one to three weeks. In just international travel costs alone, this support has been in the vicinity of $8,000.

Another opportunity for travel funds lies in organizations, either professional or charitable, of which you are a member. Frequently such groups will host travel or accommodations for either you or your group.

When traveling, have you ever missed connections or had reservation foulups, etc., that have resulted in changes in your plans? If these problems are caused by an airline company or travel agency, you can expect them to pay for overnight accomodations. Frequently they will also throw in a free day's tour of local sights. My family and I have enjoyed such "fringe benefits" in Hong Kong, Guatemala, Yucatan, and Panama, and they have been offered in Peru and Kenya. If you know your rights, you can often get extra service for the price of your original arrangements. In Yucatan, I was in charge of a tour group of twenty-five people. When our reservations on the island of Cozumel were not honored, the travel agency, at my request, coughed up our Cozumel fares and hotel expenses and then provided the group with $1,000 worth of free hotel space in Merida. In Peru, an airline offered us a day's accomodations plus a free tour if we would relinquish our reserved-seat space and travel a day later.

Grants on the other hand, are not quite free money. Normally, in order to acquire a grant you must promise to do a certain amount of work in order to get, say, 10 to 50 percent of the money you need to do what you promise to do. Therefore, contrary to popular belief, grants can actually constitute a burden rather than a boon. Nonetheless, it is possible with grant funds to acquire for your own use a salary, travel expenses, lab or field equipment, supplies, and more. The real advantage of grants is that, with the exception of salaries, none of these categories is taxable. If you are in the category of a principal investigator, then you prepare the grant request and can write in the things that you need and, occasionally, even those things that you want. However, you must be sure that the funds are spent for the specific purpose for which they were originally approved.

OPM is especially available if you wish to expand your business activities. You can establish a line of credit at a bank, take a friend in as a business partner, sell limited partnerships, or even form a corporation and sell stock. Where a bank is involved, you simply demonstrate that you have a successful track record in your business endeavor. The bank will then be willing to back you in exchange for prompt repayment plus interest. Any of the other arrangements amount to free money. The principals are willing to put up their funds in anticipation of future profits. If no profits materialize, you don't owe them any interest. They may well expect to hold a lien on their portion of the business assets, but this is only fair since their funds made the acquisition of further assets possible. Frequently partners or stockholders have a tax problem, and a temporary loss for tax purposes may actually be to their advantage. This means that it is often easier to locate someone with money to join your enterprise than it is to come up with the funds on your own.

For example, we started in the cattle business on our own in 1970. By 1971 we were facing problems of a negative cash flow. One of our friends became interested and we formed a partnership in 1971. He received a tax loss for several years, which he used to reduce his taxes. Meanwhile, the herd was increasing in size and we were building equity. In 1975 we showed a profit for the first time. In 1976 we arranged for a line of credit at the bank to buy more animals, giving us an even greater tax writeoff while not even using our own funds. To recapitulate, we started eight years ago with three cows and three calves.

Today we have eighty-five head and a $50,000 line of credit. In the meantime both we and our partner have received tax rebates, so it has been advantageous for all of us.

We also discussed forming a limited partnership to include another investor. He had sold his business and was looking for a tax-sheltered investment. We discussed buying a $20,000 imported French Limousin heifer, which we would then consign to an embryo transplanting service. For a $5,000 fee the service would operate on the heifer, remove and fertilize the ova and then transplant those into several common cows, which would carry and bear the calves normally. In this way it is possible to breed several full brothers and sisters simultaneously. When they are expensive stock, the returns can be financially very rewarding. As it turned out, we didn't proceed with the deal because of the risks of nonconception due to the possibility that the expensive female might be sterile. Nonetheless, our limited partner would have been willing to put up the funds.

If you have a good investment idea, rest assured that you can find backers willing to put up their money to support your program. In fact, as I shall discuss in another section, there are lots of people willing to buy franchises and get into other investment deals where their chances for success vary from slim to nonexistent.

The classic example of OPM is borrowing funds to carry out your investment program. One advantage is that you can acquire large amounts of leverage. A second advantage is acquiring the ability to become involved in certain investments in the first place. With OPM it is possible to engage in larger deals or those that require a longer term to mature. These are deals which, if you had to pay your own way, you couldn't swing at all. Viewed in a realistic context, OPM is your primary means to major wealth in this lifetime. Practically everyone who started with nothing and now has it made started with OPM. I have already pointed out the advantages of borrowing and leverage. Your funds are obtained tax-free, and when invested at a return greater than the interest charged, they provide a free source of income.

I won't cover the different techniques of obtaining OPM in great detail because this has already been done by Tyler G. Hicks (1970, p. 8). The formula for success that Hicks outlines is simple: (1) know who's ready to lend money, (2) understand borrowing techniques, (3) borrow for investment purposes, and (4) put OPM to work. The kinds of loans you can obtain include personal, business, compensating balance, "anything," collateral, state and federal, and sales of stocks and bonds.

For those unfamiliar with borrowing, the personal loan is the easiest to acquire and can often be obtained on a signature without the necessity of collateral. Typical provisions of a personal loan include a monthly payment of principal and interest plus, frequently, actual deduction of the interest amount at the time the loan is made (this is known as discounting). The maximum amount obtainable on a personal loan varies from $1,500 to $5,000. Personal loans can be the best first step toward an investment program because they provide considerable flexibility even though the scale is small. The principal disadvantage of a personal loan is the monthly payment. If your investment does not pay income on a monthly basis, the personal loan may work a hardship. On the other hand the personal loan can be a *means* to enforce a monthly savings plan while your investment is maturing. If your investment requires more than $5,000 it is also possible to get a personal loan from each of several banks at the same time. While the banks may not check to see if you are applying elsewhere, they will check to determine the amount of your outstanding indebtedness. Their concern is your ability to repay. It takes some fast footwork to borrow $20,000 or $30,000 on simultaneous personal loans, but if your investment can simultaneously make the payments and build equity, it can be a good deal.

The general requirements for obtaining a personal loan include having a steady job, having worked at that job for six months or more, having lived at the same address for six or more months, having a telephone, and owning an automobile or other property. The basic first steps, then, in acquiring your loan are to meet these requirements, which serve primarily to indicate that you are a permanent resident of the community and that you are dependable. If you have difficulty in establishing your credit for that first personal loan, a cosigner could make the difference. Once you acquire that first loan, then a record of prompt repayment will be your best ally.

The business loan provides much greater flexibility than a personal loan in that you can borrow to meet any kind of need.

You can acquire funds to build facilities, build inventory, hire personnel, buy materials, buy out a competitor, etc. The advantages of a business loan are several: (1) you can use your business as collateral, (2) the loans are typically for three- to twelve-month terms, and (3) they are renewable. All you need to do is to pay the interest regularly. This advantage makes it easier to keep your OPM working long enough to begin showing a profit. The pressure to repay the principal borrowed is postponed until your business has had the chance to really take off.

The compensating balance loan consists of your leaving an amount on deposit in your bank. The bank will in turn loan you up to four or five times the amount you have on deposit. The costs of such a loan are somewhat greater than other types because the bank gets to use your compensating balance instead of your using it. However, it has the advantage of making it possible to borrow several times more than you could borrow on a straight loan. Consider an apartment building requiring a $30,000 down payment. If you only have $10,000 cash, a compensating balance loan could enable you to swing the deal. The potential income on such an investment, assuming a total value in the vicinity of $300,000 with rents at one percent of the total value of the property per month, would be $36,000 per year. That would be more than enough to retire your compensating balance loan. In fact, at this rate, the rents from ten months would equal your entire loan.

The "anything" loan is simply a banker's gimmick to bring in more business. A bank will loan small amounts, up to several thousand dollars, for any purpose. The advantage to you is that you could use such a loan to get into an investment that the bank might view as too speculative for a business loan.

I have already discussed loans based on collateral in detail. Suffice it to say that once you have built up some collateral you are well on the way to becoming a successful Penny Capitalist.

Loans from state or federal sources are outstanding because they are usually at low interest rates. Often, qualifying for such a loan amounts to no more than filling out the proper forms. Such loans are frequently for business purposes and have as their reason for being the establishment of new jobs or other "public interest" features. When applying for such a loan be sure to read the application materials very carefully because the loans are made according to government-program guidelines rather than your personal needs.

The biggest problem with all of the above is that they are loans; you have to repay them at some time, plus interest. As an alternative, the capitalist system has developed the sale of corporate stock as a means of raising venture capital. The steps involved are relatively easy, and the proceeds are tuned to the needs of the new business rather than the needs or requirements of a lender.

Supercurrency:* OPM in Spades

In many ways the sale of stock is *the* device for raising capital. Funds derived from stock sales never have to be repaid, are tax-free, are interest-free, and can be used for any business purpose. Your only obligation under such a plan is that you must form a corporation and conform with the rules of your state and/or those of the federal Securities and Exchange Commission with respect to the sale of stock. Furthermore, you are under the moral obligation to pay dividends to the stockholders when your corporation finally earns a profit. When you sell stock to the public, they become part-owners in your corporation. In exchange for the free loan of their funds it is only fair that some return be paid when it is available. However, in the normal course of events you as the corporate organizer retain control of the company. Therefore, you have the freedom to either reinvest profits in the business or pay dividends; the choice is yours, not the stockholders'.

When selling stock to the public you must first form your corporation, then prepare a prospectus that outlines your company's history, lists its officers, and gives its legal address, the amount in its treasury, a record of its earnings, a description

---

* This term was coined by "Adam Smith" (1972, p. 15), and it means *capitalized income.*

of the company's product or activities, and other relevant data. You must then register with the SEC your intent to sell stock and conform to their rules and the rules of the state in which your corporation is registered. You can carry out the actual sale of stock yourself, or you can get a brokerage firm to do it for you.

The major advantages of "going public" through a stock sale are many: (1) You share the risk with other shareholders. (2) You raise the capital you need, tax-free. (3) You retain control of the company. (4) You can retain sufficient shares to give you fantastic leverage when the share price rises. (I have already discussed how Oceanic Exploration, with no income and $700,000 in debts, probably made multi-millionaires out of its principal shareholders simply through the sale of shares to the public.)

If you have a corporation you may also obtain the funds you need by issuing bonds. This is a fairly sophisticated level of financial involvement and doesn't really fit the modus operandi of the Penny Capitalist. However, I will mention it here briefly in the interest of fully covering our subject. When a corporation sells bonds it borrows from the public for a fixed length of time at a fixed rate of interest. One advantage of this is that your debt obligations are known from the beginning and you can budget for their repayment. Further, such funds are obtained tax-free and then repaid out of pretax earnings. Finally, and perhaps most important, the issuance of bonds does not dilute the ownership of the company. When you sell stock you sell a percentage of ownership of the company; the sale of bonds raises money just as easily, but keeps complete ownership in your hands. In any case, the sale of stocks or bonds makes it possible to raise tax-free funds at the discretion of the entre-preneur without the interference of some lending agency. And if your company fails, the risks are assumed by the stock- and bondholders. You are not legally obligated personally to repay the debts of your corporation. In a corporate bankruptcy, the corporation's assets are distributed on a proportional basis to the bondholders first and then, if anything remains, to the stockholders.

Supercurrency, in "Adam Smith's" terms, is the printing and selling of stock in a corporation in order to finance your operations. As Smith explains (1972), the real fortunes are made by going public with an already successful private firm. Often a family business has expanded and various family members, who may no longer be active in managing the firm, wish to exchange their interests for cash. Selling stock to the public is one way to do this while continuing to maintain total control. The Ford Motor Company is the classic example of a family firm going public with the founding family still remaining in the drivers's seat—and that's a pun!

Frequently such an approach makes it possible for a family to have its cake and eat it too. An example is the public offering of Montford of Colorado in 1974. A family-owned meat-packing and cattle-feeding business, Montford had become one of the giants of the industry while still remaining in family owner-ship. The stock was offered at about fifteen dollars a share, and went up slightly to sixteen or so, and then sold off slightly. Shortly thereafter meat-price controls were imposed by the gov-ernment, and some four years later the meat industry is still recovering from ruinous economic conditions. Today Montford is selling at five and a half. If we suppose that the family mem-bers kept the cash they acquired four years ago, they could buy back today the same percentage interest they sold in 1974 for one-third of its former value. Such manipulations with super-currency are common and permit the really wealthy to live a lifestyle somewhat different from that of you and me. Mean-while, even though we may recognize the value of supercur-rency, its utilization is largely limited to either the real capi-talists or charlatans. Its utility for the Penny Capitalist seems somewhat minimal at this point. What is necessary to deal in supercurrency is first to build up a successful business.

Cost-Sharing

Cost-sharing is another boondoggle. Numerous federal agen-cies have programs under which either approved project ex-penses are met on a share basis or loans can be acquired to help fund a project. These loans are either at lower-than-average interest rates or guaranteed by a federal agency in case of default, or both. Most of my experience is in the agricultural programs, where it is possible to share-cost on land leveling, terracing, pond building, reseeding, irrigation canal lining, etc. Another major source of funds is the Small Business Administration. All of these programs have specific rules and conditions, and if you can meet the conditions, funds are normally approved. My neighbor received a cost-sharing grant from the state's game and fish department in addition to federal help when he built his stock ponds.

One of the largest cost-sharing programs of all is the Bureau of Land Management's program under the Taylor Grazing Act. Under that program it is possible to lease federal lands for livestock grazing. The fees are about $1.40 a month per animal unit. Comparable grazing on private land costs about eight dollars a month per animal unit. The difference in those costs represents a federal subsidy to those lucky enough to have a grazing lease. My purpose here is not to itemize or justify every kind of cost-sharing program in existence. I am simply suggesting that if you look around you may well find some such program that will help you do what you are planning to do anyway. If someone else puts up part of the cost, so much the better.

Although they are not usually thought of as such, tax deductions, credits, and rebates also constitute a form of cost-sharing. Think about it.

Free Services

"Free" services are not really OPM, but they fill the same bill. Lots of free services exist, and some may help you down the path to financial stability. Real estate agents appraise property; bankers and other loan officers will discuss your investment plans with you; and insurance agents will arrange your coverage to best meet your needs. Brokers don't charge for their advice; they only receive commissions when you actually buy or sell something. An amazing amount of investment advice is free, and you should avail yourself of it. Usually your sources are trying to sell you something, a retirement-community condominium, a mutual fund, gold bars, etc. No matter what their pitch, you have the opportunity to listen to what they say and form your own opinions. Several years ago I attended an evening seminar on investments in gold put on by a syndicate that had for sale anything you wanted: gold bullion, gold coins, shares in gold-mining companies. Their salesman was young and enthusiastic. His charts and graphs showed the price of gold would skyrocket soon after it was legal for Americans to own gold. Even if the price didn't hold, his alternative graph showed gold fluctuating mildly before resuming its upward movement. The actual history since then has been somewhat different from his predictions. Those who already owned gold sold and took their profits. Sellers included some national governments, and the price of gold declined to about $120 an ounce from its prelegalization price of $200. So far the young man was dead wrong in his predicted price action, but nonetheless, it was an interesting evening—and it was free. Meanwhile, at this writing, the price of gold seems to have bottomed out at about $120 to $128, and now that the hoopla is over, it is moving back up.

Probably the greatest variety and greatest value in free services are provided by federal agencies. There are VA loans. HUD provides help in rebuilding slum areas and in construction of low-cost housing. County agricultural agents provide expertise in all forms of agricultural services. The list goes on and on. There are undoubtedly many such programs that I know nothing about, and it would be to your advantage to find out about them.

There are those who complain bitterly that government funds are wasted on innumerable giveaway programs. I agree with them. However, it's a fact of life that such programs exist, and they benefit those who apply. In the absence of any real governmental reform (despite recent events in California and elsewhere, don't hold your breath!), one can either gripe or get on the gravy train. The choice is yours.

Some Minor Sources of OPM

Another source of OPM consists of charging items purchased on the thirty-day credit plans offered by various businesses. If you pay within thirty days no interest is charged. It is a way to modestly stretch your buying power, but is no real substitute for creative borrowing. The same may be said for the savings plans that permit you interest payments from the first of the month for funds deposited any day up to the tenth of the month. Unless you have large sums to deposit, such gambits don't really amount to much. The same may be said for the free gifts handed out for deposits in savings institutions. If they can afford the gifts, you can find a better place for your investable funds.

There are incongruities in the use of OPM. If you borrow a small amount on a personal loan your credit record will be closely examined. On the other hand, you can sell stocks or bonds for large amounts without any real credit check. Probably the key to the whole system is thinking big. If you think big the system has the means to fulfill your needs. But even if you think small, the system can take care of that too.

12

Investment Pitfalls

Numerous authors have remarked on the ease with which hard-working, long-saving individuals will relinquish their funds to invest in schemes about which they know little or nothing. In many cases they are victims of their own greed. In other situations they appear almost to be gambling. They have worked so long and so hard for so little that they eventually plunge in with all they have in hopes of making a killing. The opposite is almost always the case; they either lose all they invest, or the investment pays off so poorly that their funds would have returned more from a savings account.

In many cases such individuals are the victims of fast-buck conmen who have no intention of paying off on any investment. They simply have a story to sell, and once they have made a sale, they decamp for parts unknown. The come-on is usually an ad in a local newspaper that states that a national company is looking for distributors in the area. The ad further implies that substantial financial returns can be obtained for a minimal investment of both time and funds. Credit references are also required. If the ad is answered, a salesman will call and discuss the opportunity, which usually turns out to be selling brushes, soaps, cosmetics, nuts, candy, etc., door-to-door or through vending machines. The routine pitch requires a cash investment on the part of the victim for the machines, the merchandise, or both. The victim is normally promised company help in establishing a clientele. Once on the hook the victim may never even receive the soap or whatever he has supposedly purchased. Even if the goods are received they usually have been marked up to an exorbitant level and may well be unsaleable. In short, there is no market for the merchandise and there may be no company to back the promises made.

I have had the good fortune to sit through one of these sales pitches, and I can report that it conformed in every way to those described in print (Margolius 1971). My parents were looking for a second retirement income and had answered such an ad. The salesman appeared on schedule and described the advantages of selling hot nuts out of his company's machines. The cost was only $500 for the machines, and the salesman would help set up the sales route. Fortunately, I was home from college and talked my parents out of the deal, as it was obvious that the money-making potential was purely speculative. The salesman called back once but made no further effort to encourage my parents to go into business. It was clear that the salesman was only interested in the one-time sales commission.

The Fast-Franchise Syndrome

Another major gimmick in recent years has been franchising. For a cash investment you can become the operator of the local outlet of an established fast-food chain or discount store. The idea is that these deals are finger lickin' good all the way to the bank. There are indeed valid money-making opportunities in franchising. There have also been numerous scams. These fraudulent deals have tended to operate in two ways. The first of these may result from overenthusiasm rather than out and out fraud. The chain operators plan to operate a national chain but lack financing and other requisites. The result is that the store is never built or if it comes into operation the products promised are overpriced and of low quality, with the result that customer acceptance evaporates.

The second danger to would-be entrepreneurs stems from company organization. Numerous companies sell distributorships that provide a sales commission to those farther up the chain of command. Such distributorships are therefore a hierarchy of governors, generals, and chairmen of the board, each of whom has paid a graduated fee and each of whom is to

receive a commission for each new distributor recruited at a level below him. There is a chainletter or pyramid aspect to these organizations, which relies on the recruiting of more distributors for profits rather than on the sale of products. Usually the distributors end up with a basement full of soap or cosmetics with no one to buy the stuff. The best known of these operations, such as Glenn Turner's "Dare to be Great" and Koscot Cosmetics, have ended up in court.

In short, franchises are not investments—even the legitimate ones. The legitimate franchises require long hours of hard work to make them pay off. Therefore they are not investments in the true sense of return based on the use of capital. They are businesses. The fraudulent franchise deals only compound the problem since they aren't investments either, but simply con games.

Mutual Funds: Panacea or Ripoff?

Mutual funds have been touted as the means for the small investor to partake of the benefits of capitalism, a method of investing on a shoestring and simultaneously having your funds in the care of professional management. The public has bought this sales pitch to the tune of a 2,100 percent increase in fund assets between 1950 and 1970, from $2.5 billion to $55 billion (Springer 1973, p. 6). Meanwhile, investments in fixed-income-producing cash-value life insurance declined over the same term from 42 percent of Americans' savings to a bare 20 percent. Appraisal of these trends suggests that Americans have become more selective in their investments and have deliberately selected the inflation hedge and capital growth opportunities offered by the mutual funds to the detriment of the life insurance industry.

Mutual funds also have the proclaimed virtues of diversification, as a means to minimize risk, and specializing in type, which gives one a broad-based investment in a specific market area, e.g., atomic development, undersea exploration, new issues, over-the-counter stocks, bonds, etc. It is therefore possible to shop for funds much in the same way one shops for individual stocks or bonds. The larger fund holdings permit diversification and "bargain" commission rates not available to the small investor on his own.

If we put all of these advantages together, diversification, professional management, and lower commissions, the mutual funds should out-perform the market. Numerous authorities, however, have provided evidence that such has not been the case. In general, the market averages have out-performed the funds. An overall appraisal is that the funds have out-performed the averages on an up market, but have sunk more rapidly than the averages in a down market. However, on balance, the averages have out-performed the funds. Furthermore, there is evidence that even in good years some funds have turned in lackluster performances, and in bad years some of the funds were dreadful, losing up to 50 percent of their quoted assets.

What has gone wrong with this utopian investment medium? The SEC has investigated mutual funds and reports several inherent problems in their operating procedures. Of significance has been their initial sales fee, averaging 8 percent, which has often resulted in little or no gain for the investor during the first year. Where the initial sums invested are part of a contractual investment plan to extend over a number of years, the initial year investment may be cut in half by the sales charge assessed for the entire plan. A second problem has been excessive churning of accounts, resulting in brokerage commissions exceeding the gain in equity. A further problem, and perhaps the most serious, is that analysis of the performance of stocks after they have been bought or sold by the funds indicates that often the fund managers were wrong in their buy-and-sell decisions. In short, analysis suggests that management has been guilty of malfeasance in its assigned professional responsibility. Part of the record of the late 1960s included a shift by the funds to complete reliance on performance rather than safety of principal. These so-called go-go funds boomed after 1965, only to fall apart in the 1969–70 debacle. With performance becoming the object, stocks were bought and almost immediately sold if they didn't live up to expectations.

Two further factors turned this period into a prolonged horror movie. Simultaneously with the shift to performance on the part of the mutual funds, the corporate world discovered creative accounting. Assets of no or dubious value were reassessed on the firms' balance sheets. Assets of companies yet to be bought were counted toward current income, as were the projected incomes of facilities not yet brought into production. Creative accounting led to constantly rising earnings per share or, in a bad year, to all the bad news being released at once, causing the stock to plunge like a rock. Finally, the mutual funds became victims of their own huge size. They tended to concentrate their activities in a few stocks, such as the top 500 corporations, since the smaller corporations had too few shares outstanding to provide a safe medium for buying and selling. In addition, the mutual fund orders were so large, involving sales and purchases of lots of 100,000 to 300,000 shares, that when a fund placed an order it couldn't be executed. Also, the large order modified the market price during its execution so that neither buying nor selling could be conducted at the desired price. Both practices shaved fund profits.

Another gambit of the mutual funds was the establishment of "fund funds." Such funds would buy only shares of other mutual funds and therefore achieve the ultimate in diversification and presumably the lowest element of risk. Actually, these funds were proclaimed by the SEC to be essentially without merit. They compounded the total management fees charged as well as the commissions on buying and selling. In fact, it often occurred that one of the held funds would sell a particular stock at the same time that another such fund would buy the same stock. The net result for the investor was an equity status quo minus buy and sell commissions.

Mutual funds are not all bad. Most investors participate in them whether they choose to or not as a result of their ownership in pension plans and insurance investments. What seems relevant to the Penny Capitalist is that mutual funds as builders of equity have been greatly overpromoted. A further problem concerns the redemption rate. Years ago I told the first mutual fund salesman I met that I saw two problems with funds: (1) the investor did not own his shares in industry outright, and (2) there would come a market crash some day in which the small mutual-fund investor couldn't redeem his shares and get out soon enough. This actually happened in 1969, and even though the small investor was able to redeem his shares, the funds were unable to sell their large losers and had to ride the market down. As a result the redemptions were at a low level. The time for selected mutual funds in your portfolio seems to me to be when you have accumulated your basic capital and wish to diversify to reduce your risk. Then a mutual fund investment may well make sense.

Fixed-Dollar Investments

Investments that pay interest on a fixed invested amount have over the recent bull market, which began in 1948, been rather poor performers for the investor. Traditionally, such investments have included bonds, life insurance, savings bonds, and interest-bearing savings accounts. The problem with these investments has been their lack of compensation for the reduction in buying power resulting from inflation. Their promoters have proclaimed their safety as their outstanding asset, to the extent that frequently the interest paid has even been at less than current rates. Advertisements such as that of a local savings

220

and loan company, "No depositor has ever suffered a loss," are not only misleading but probably could also be challenged in court. However, I must be clear here in stating that fixed-dollar investments can be your best haven during times of deflation. It is during inflation that they become the sly pickpocket. During inflation the loss of buying power plus income tax on the interest received combine to make it impossible for fixed-income investments to meet the twin goals of safety of principal and a reasonable return.

Beyond the loss of buying power resulting from inflation are two other major villains that tend to reduce the income from fixed-dollar investments. One is the overconservatism of the managers of the investments for insurance companies and pension plans. Their concern for safety leads them to sacrifice potential income. The second problem concerns the fine print in direct investment in fixed-income situations. Often interest-bearing accounts or bonds pay lower interest for shorter terms. In addition, in some cases, unless the funds are left on deposit for the specified term no interest at all may be paid, and the bank or bond issuer has had free use of your funds. Such interest pinching is sometimes a deliberate part of an investment program, and investors are led to believe they will receive interest that in fact is not part of the agreement. Now do you understand why if you borrow $1,000 from your bank for a year it costs you $100 plus, but if you deposit $1,000 in a savings account there your return may be only $40 or so even if the bank promises more?

Another bummer is interest penalties. Stated in baldest terms, interest penalties are interest charges imposed after a loan has been repaid. A common clause in mortgage agreements provides for a prepayment penalty. During times of inflation the lender gets repaid immediately if you sell or refinance. He then reinvests these funds at a higher interest rate; at the same time he socks you with an interest penalty. As we have already seen, these charges are added to an amortization schedule that includes payment of more interest than principal during the early life of the mortgage. Don't expect that these unfair practices will cease or be reduced by so-called truth-in-lending legislation. Just be prepared to ferret out such interest-pinching language the next time you shop for a mortgage.

Finally, I want to include a word about charges for nonser-

221

vices. Such charges include points assessed on new mortgages, mortgage assumption fees, and brokerage fees charged for account churning, i.e., any charge for which the investor does not receive corresponding service or value. The world is full of these rigged deals that benefit only the riggers. The only advice I can give in this area is to know your lenders and exact the most value for your money that you possibly can. Even real estate commissions fall into this category. The average real estate agent expects to show you three properties in a two-hour period and have you buy one of them so he can collect his $1,000 to $2,000 commission. Make him work for what he gets!

Segal's Law

Now a word about sales resistance. In general, the more highly advertised anything is, the less chance there is that it is a genuine investment. This rule pertains to sales of mini-ranchettes, that retirement or ski condominium, an isolated bit of beach in the Caribbean, penny stocks on the Canadian exchange, silver commemorative plates, mutual funds, tax shelters in real estate or cattle, etc. All of these "opportunities" fit Segal's law. Joe Segal, founder of the Lincoln Mint, has stated, "The more a plate or other limited-edition product is promoted for its investment value, the less that value is likely to be" (Randall 1973, p. 38). Segal should know; he has lined up 600,000 of those Mr. Barnum said were born at the rate of one a minute. I believe Segal was too restrictive when he confined his law to "limited-edition" products. I believe that *any* investment fits his law. The more any item is promoted for its investment value, the less that value is likely to be. Think about it; how often have you seen ads for some retirement subdivision and then happened to drive by it or one like it on your summer vacation? Were you surprised to see street signs propped up by tumbleweeds and no one living there? Flying over those subdivisions is even more revealing. Miles and miles of checkerboard roads bulldozed out of an otherwise empty desert do not an investment make.

A colleague of mine in the Air Force signed up to buy four lots in such a subdivision in Florida. Advertised in the *Air Force Times*, with an artist's drawing of a future retirement com-

Segal's law in action

munity, the project was fifteen miles inland from Ft. Myers in reclaimed swamp land. At $500 a lot, he bought four, which totaled, as I remember, about an acre. This was in 1954, so the prices weren't all that cheap. I asked him why he bought four lots. He answered that that was the most he could afford on the installment plan. It would be interesting to learn how his "investment" has fared. My simple dictum on such things is: If it's advertised as an investment, watch out.

By contrast, for back taxes I bought three acres located in Western Ontario, four miles from the shore of Lake Superior. The land was advertised as tax-delinquent property for sale, not as an "investment." The property is a corner lot that has recently been incorporated into the limits of a city of 100,000. I have owned it ten years, and it has increased in value about twenty times. Our initial cost was $180, so our risk was minimal. Now there is an investment! Meanwhile our taxes are about six dollars a year.

Selling Too Cheaply

Another pitfall is selling too cheaply. I have discussed the difficulty of judging when to sell. Even when prices on what you own are quoted daily it is difficult to decide on the proper time to sell. Selling is even more difficult when what you have is a unique object and no one knows what it is really worth. If you have such an object, my advice is to proceed slowly. Simply because you haven't located a buyer doesn't mean that your price is too high. Remember the painting the Antique Lady bought from the Fastest Trader in the West that immediately resold for a 237 percent profit. He sold too cheaply because he misjudged the market. The painting was worth what he first asked. When he didn't immediately locate a buyer he panicked and cut his price. Don't follow his example. Sometimes the best way to get a buyer's attention may even be *raising* your price. He may pass up that Mongolian bedpan at $50, but if it is priced at $500 and on sale at $350, he may snatch it up as a bargain.

A variant of this same approach concerns pricing your services. Just because you invest little time in a project doesn't mean that what you have done isn't valuable. I once engaged

224

a statistics student to compare the progeny data on the off-spring of two purebred bulls that I planned to use in artificial breeding. One was priced at fifteen dollars an ampule and the other at twenty-five. The computer run on the data indicated the bulls were essentially identical in their performance capability. Since the Cattle Baron owned the fifteen-dollar bull, I realized this information would be valuable to him. In fact it might help him realize $15,000 to $20,000 more if he chose to sell his bull. I offered him my results in exchange for semen from his bull. He agreed, and I picked up $750 worth of semen. My cost was $100 for the student's time.

A disappointing example of underpricing one's value involves a colleague of mine. He is a world-famous scholar who contracted to write a book for a major publisher. He received a cash settlement of $8,000. The book was well received, and 3 million copies were sold at four dollars each. Had my friend insisted on a royalty contract, he would have received $500,000 or more for his efforts. Don't emulate his example!

Summing up:

- Beware of overpromotion in the sale of any security or investment opportunity.

- Beware of franchises and pyramid-type organizations.

- Investigate your interest-bearing opportunities to determine if the interest promised will be the interest you will receive.

- Avoid or minimize, where you are legally trapped, charges for nonservice.

- Don't sell too cheaply; value what you have to offer and the buyer will too.

- View mutual funds with a jaundiced eye.

- Above all, remember Segal's law.

Regulation Q and You

If you have ever wondered why savings accounts pay such low interest, you can blame Regulation Q. This is a rule established by the U.S. government that limits the legal rate of interest

Regulation Q in action

commercial banks and savings and loan companies can pay small savers. These rates are 5 percent at commercial banks and 5.25 percent at savings and loan companies. The rates were established in 1966 to make available to these lending institutions a cheap source of home-mortgage money. Since 1966 large savers have been able to earn substantially more on their time deposits, up to a high of 9.9 percent on Treasury bills in 1974, for example. However, the joker in the deck is that the higher rates of interest are only available to those with megabucks, $10,000 or more, to invest. With inflation averaging more than 6 percent a year, you can see how the small saver has been penalized. In fact, it is estimated that since 1966 the total loss suffered by small savers at the hands of Regulation Q has been $30 billion. What is unfair about this arrangement is that small savers are subsidizing home-mortgage owners, and in many cases, these represent different segments of our population. We need reform in this area, and Representative Henry S. Reuss of Wisconsin has introduced legislation in Congress to do just that. If you have medical insurance and credit at your local lender's office so that you can get a loan in an emergency, you don't really need that savings account anyway. Stop being victimized by forces beyond your control. Withdraw your savings and invest them where they will generate a return greater than the current rate of inflation.

227

13

A Comprehensive Profile of the Penny Capitalist

The advice I have outlined in this book and the examples I have used were selected to provide a philosophical approach to investments and investing when you don't have any real capital to operate with. The problem then is twofold: how to acquire your initial capital and how to invest small amounts for a rapid return in order to build your capital sufficiently to change your lifestyle and provide for future needs.

I have suggested that a special set of practices and a unique point of view are essential in order to achieve these goals. The successful Penny Capitalist must recognize that the bulk of all investment literature and advice is not for him because it is aimed at those who already have substantial resources to invest. As a Penny Capitalist, you must develop your own plan for investment action. Your buy-and-sell decisions must be based on your own appraisal of current and future market actions. The rules governing your conduct are easy to state, but they are difficult to practice, as they require personality traits that are not common. The standard investment caveats are not for the Penny Capitalist. Your problem is simple: If you begin with nothing, conservative investments will not pay off soon enough for you to enjoy the proceeds in a single lifetime. You must strive in the initial years of your program for a rate of return that approximates a 50 to 100 percent increase in equity per year. Several years into the program more conservative investments may be contemplated, those returning between 15 and 50 percent a year. (By *return* I mean an increase in equity;

an increase in income is self-defeating because of our "progressive" tax structure.)

In order to make your initial investments it is imperative to buy something, no matter how little it costs. It is also imperative that such purchases be made out of existing family income. This means that the entire family budget should be scrutinized to determine how funds may be diverted into investments. At the same time, means must be explored to increase your present buying power through reliance on garage sales and other cheap sources of consumer commodities. The basis of both increasing your buying power and making shrewd investments is the distinction between buying at retail and buying at wholesale or below. Buying below wholesale is recommended as the essential ingredient in both rapid acquisition of equity and being able to easily resell at a profit. The search for bargains then becomes a regular and consistent ingredient in the lifestyle of the Penny Capitalist. It is both a challenging game and a financially rewarding avocation. Furthermore, the search for bargains adds more than an increase in equity for the future; it also provides a more satisfying life as you go along.

Basic ingredients of the formula include buying nonliquid investments that build equity rapidly but that are not quickly convertible to cash. Such a limitation provides the incentive to maintain an equity position rather than to sell out and pay current bills. Another major ingredient is the ability to maximize the investment potential of your funds by using leverage. The ideal leverage is provided by mortgaging out to the extent that you have none of your cash invested but still retain an equity position. Techniques that make such activities possible include getting the seller to carry part of the balance, refinancing, trading equities that you can't sell, or taking an equity interest in exchange for your services in lieu of a sales commission. Buying at a level below wholesale provides instant equity inasmuch as you may then finance the entire existing balance. No matter which technique you use, the acquisition of equities is the essential first step in the accumulation of capital.

Because of the pitfalls along the way and the plethora of inadequate or inappropriate advice, it is essential to become your own investment expert. You cannot depend on others to manage your affairs with an expectation of above-average results, and you must achieve above-average results in order to reach your goals. When shopping for investment bargains you must have the ability to recognize value when you see it, and when you determine that such value is underpriced, buy. Such competence must be developed to the extent that a decision can be made on the spot. Frequently there is no time to consult references or authorities. Becoming your own expert is the only margin of safety that you have. If you don't buy a bargain on the spot, don't expect to be able to come back for it later; someone else will have already picked it up.

When buying, shop carefully for mortgage terms. It is possible to buy equities with none of your own funds invested. The nothing-ventured-something-gained technique is a powerful mechanism for the rapid accumulation of capital.

Remember that lending institutions indulge in self-deception when it comes to examining financial statements. If your financial statement looks good, they may fail to peek beneath the surface. If they believe you to be worth more, they will be willing to loan you more. To improve your financial statement, pick up an equity for little or nothing, list the equity as a valuable asset, then pyramid its potential further by using it as collateral for a loan or as part of your net assets increasing your overall financial worth. Such assets are therefore of value in strengthening your image as a good credit risk.

Don't forget the power of cash. In certain situations even a little bit of cash may be all it takes to close a favorable deal. Manage your credit in such a way that it works for you instead of against you. Such creative borrowing will ease your way to the things you want out of life.

All investments are related to the status of the marketplace. Things of investment quality vary greatly in price depending on the current status of the market and their recognized value. What exists, then, is a fluctuating scenario against which shrewd buys in advance of price rises can pay off immensely. Step one in this campaign is to look for real value. If it is there and the item is priced low, the normal course of events will cause its price to be higher at a later date. In general, the best

230

The Penny Capitalist's plan for investment action

investments are those that are least recognized as such at the time of purchase. Conversely, the more an item is advertised for its investment value, the less likely that value will be there.

The next step in playing the market is to constantly reappraise the potential for increase in price of the items that you hold. If the price fails to go up or looks as though it has hit a stage of diminishing potential for increase, sell. Selling is always easiest at the height of enthusiasm. This is when most buyers believe that the future is even brighter. Such selling is quick and easy. Once the peak of enthusiasm is past you may be able to sell at the same price, but your downside risk has increased and it may take much longer to find an interested buyer. Selling is easy if you bought at a favorable price. Some don'ts include not trying to get top dollar and not trying to pinpoint the top of the market. If you can sell out at a fair profit, sell. Only hang on for a greater return if you are convinced that the market is going substantially higher. Remember, you can sell anything, even a bar of soap wrapped in a dollar bill.

Keeping what you have earned is the greatest challenge of modern life. It is a fight to the finish between you and the IRS as far as the accumulation of your capital is concerned. Our tax structure has evolved to maintain the status quo and to keep money in circulation. You don't want to put your money back in circulation; you want to keep it. Therefore you are engaged, whether you wish to be or not, in a life-and-death struggle with the powerful interests that draft and enforce the various forms of taxation, including the hidden taxes of inflation. Numerous techniques are on your side. You may increase your buying power through internal methods—for example, setting aside a tax-sheltered retirement account and reducing your living costs through shopping at garage sales. A critical idea is that $1.00 saved is $1.25 earned. Refinancing can produce tax-free cash, and charitable contributions can reduce your tax liabilities.

The most flexible tax savings can be affected through business expenditures. Herein lies the true gold at the end of the rainbow. Through depreciation, the investment tax-credit, and standard operating deductions it is possible to own or to do many of the things you desire at a reduction in cost of 25 percent or better. The ultimate trip is to convert what you have to shares of stock, sell out at the right time, and thereby reduce the tax imposed to that at the capital gains rate.

In your initial investments it is wise to recognize that the organized markets—securities, coins, stamps, and the like—provide the least opportunity for profit. Sleepers are hard to find because of the wide range of information available to buyers and sellers. At the same time, the information available is manipulated by professionals to their advantage. Realizing these limitations, the Penny Capitalist is advised to seek out lesser-known avenues for investment. These fields may be simply unknown at present, or they may be far out in left field. In either case, if your initial cost is low, what have you got to lose? And remember, some of the greatest percentage returns discussed in this book have been acquired in the offbeat market. Organized markets are best left alone until you have your capital accumulated.

Your investments will pyramid faster if you utilize other peoples money whenever possible. You can cut your living costs or reduce your investment risk if you consistently rely on OPM. Mortgages are a primary source of OPM, as are grants and expense accounts. Taking in a limited partner is another good technique. OPM is further augmented by this tax-saving feature: not being earned income, OPM is nontaxable. In most cases, OPM is a result of someone else having a tax problem. In initiating a tax-sheltered venture you may be providing a service to others as well as doing yourself a favor.

As I have discussed above, the art of selling is essential to the establishment of a successful investment program. Techniques other than simple transactions for cash are frequently vital in making sales. Barter is a form of tax-free exchange that is often attractive to both buyer and seller. Selling on commission is another way to profit without taking any risk. Whatever is sold increases your equity position, whereas the owner still has his funds tied up in the unsold items. When you take a commission in goods of like kind or barter for other goods, your tax liability can be further reduced. The essential point is that through barter and other forms of two- or three-way exchanges items not saleable for cash may be converted to other forms of equity investment.

Timing is essential in judging the market. The time to buy

233

and the time to sell critically influence the rate at which your investments increase in value. A failure in timing can lead to long periods of time in which your funds are tied up with little or no chance for a return on your investment, much less any increase in capital.

Pitfalls to be avoided by the Penny Capitalist are both visible and hidden. The hidden pitfalls are most often of the interest-pinching, account-churning variety. The losses to the investor are not such as to wipe out his capital or even to decrease his apparent earnings to an alarming level. The villains are seldom caught because they cast a broad net and only skim off the smaller fish. Nonetheless, such pitfalls are crucial when your goal is to increase your capital at the fastest possible compound rate. In our scale of pitfalls, mutual funds would lie midway between those termed minor and those major. Mutual funds provide an excellent opportunity for their proponents to obscure the forest with trees. It takes a shrewd investor to pick a fund that is performing well above the market. Even here, past performance is not necessarily the key to future performance. The mutual fund front-end load (service charge) plus the tendency for poor-performing stocks to cancel out the good performers leads mutual funds to promise more to the investor than they deliver. Such self-deception has caused mutual funds to end up in this book under the category of investment pitfalls for the Penny Capitalist.

Finally, there are the outright bad buys—silver schlock, franchises, desert subdivisions, etc. These are investments in name only; their principal purpose is to generate sales for the salesmen. The unwanted byproduct for the would-be investor is often a basementful of unsaleable detergent or cosmetics. My suggested remedy for such pitfalls is to buy equities that are appraised prior to purchase for their present and future value. This conservative approach will avoid buying anyone's promises of future sales or future performance. After all, if you buy someone's promise and they leave you holding the bag, what have you left? True equities are repositories of real value, and they are what you should buy.

Here, in brief, are the fundamental principles of Penny Capitalism:

- An investment is whatever increases in its equity value over a period of time. Any other definition must be qualified by what has happened to the buying power of the funds originally invested.

- Buy something, no matter how little it costs.

- Buy equities of real value.

- Become your own expert on appraisal and buying.

- Buy at wholesale or below wholesale. Cut your living costs and increase your buying power by wise shopping at garage sales and other discount sources.

- Get something for nothing whenever you can.

- Be aware of the power of cash.

- Learn to borrow the maximum at the lowest possible cost.

- Manage your credit through creative borrowing.

- Learn when and how to sell. Remember, you can sell anything.

- But if you can't sell, trade.

- If you can't sell or trade, keep what you have for a possible future market.

- Divert some of your income into a tax-sheltered retirement plan.

- A dollar saved is a $1.25 earned.

- Whenever possible develop your own tax shelters.

- Become knowledgeable in offbeat investments.

- Leave participation in the organized markets for after you have accumulated your capital, when you are a "Nickel Capitalist."

- Cut your costs by using OPM.

- Avoid highly promoted "investment" opportunities.

- Keep alert for interest-pinching and other nasties.

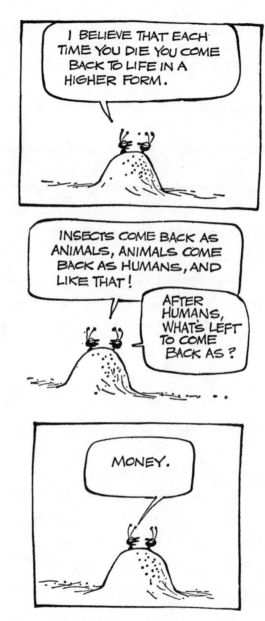

Antediluvian view of capital accumulation

- Time your buying and selling to achieve the maximum increase in your equities.

- Plan on taking twenty years to build your capital up to the higher multiples.

- Remember that the bulk of all investment advice is not for you.

- Remember that whether you are rich or poor, it is nice to have money.

A Final Word

At some point, the inflationary conditions to which the advice in *The Penny Capitalist* is tailored will end, and we will enter a period of deflation. When that happens, this book will no longer be of much use to you. A new set of techniques will have to be employed to prevent erosion of the capital you have accumulated as a Penny Capitalist. Timing your investment decisions to make the most of this transition from inflation to deflation will then be the greatest challenge you will face. I hope you will go forth and do well.

References

Baruch, Bernard, *My Own Story*, New York, Henry Holt, 1957.

Browne, Harry, *How You Can Profit from the Coming Devaluation*, New Rochelle, N.Y., Arlington House, 1970.

Emory, E. S., *When to Sell Stocks*, Homewood, Ill., Dow Jones–Irwin, 1973.

Fowler, Elizabeth M., *How to Manage Your Money*, Boston, Little, Brown, 1973.

Gilbert, W. E., *How to Profit from the Coming Land Boom in the Caribbean Islands and Latin America*, New York, Frederick Fell, 1973.

Graham, Benjamin, *The Intelligent Investor*, New York, Harper and Row, 1973.

Hazard, J. W. and L. G. Coit, *The Kiplinger Book on Investing for the Years Ahead*, Garden City, N.Y., Doubleday, 1962.

Hicks, Tyler G., *How to Borrow Your Way to a Great Fortune*, West Nyack, N.Y., Parker, 1970.

Keen, Geraldine, *Money and Art*, New York, G. P. Putnam's Sons, 1971.

Loeb, Gerald M., *The Battle for Investment Survival*, New York, Simon and Schuster, 1975.

Main, Jeremy, "Tax Shelters for the Not-So-Rich," *Money*, June 1976, pp. 73–77.

Margolius, Sidney, *The Innocent Investor and the Shaky Ground Floor*, New York, Trident, 1971.

Nicely, Glen, *How to Reap Riches from Raw Land*, Englewood Cliffs, N.J., Prentice-Hall, 1974.

Persons, J. H., Jr., *The Investor's Encyclopedia of Gold, Silver and Other Precious Metals*, New York, Random House, 1974.

Randall, Robert M., "Perils of a Mail Order Midas," *Money*, January 1973, pp. 34–38.

Reuss, Henry S., "A Fair Deal for the Small Saver," *Money*, September 1976, pp. 100–4.

Ringer, Robert J., *Winning through Intimidation*, New York, Funk and Wagnalls, 1974.

Rukeyser, Louis, *How to Make Money on Wall Street*, Garden City, N.Y., Doubleday, 1974.

Rush, Richard, *Art As an Investment*, Englewood Cliffs, N.J., Prentice-Hall, 1961.

Scheinman, W. X., *Why Most Investors Are Mostly Wrong Most of the Time*, New York, Weybright and Talley, 1970.

Schulman, M., *Anyone Can Make a Million*, Scarborough, Ont., McGraw-Hill Ryerson, 1971.

————, *Anyone Can Still Make a Million*, New York, Bantam, 1972.

"Smith, Adam," *Super Money*, New York, Popular Library, 1972.

Springer, John L., *The Mutual Fund Trap*, Chicago, Henry Regnery, 1973.

Stern, Philip M., *The Rape of the Taxpayer*, New York, Random House, 1973.

"Stocks for the Times of Your Life," *Money*, April 1974, pp. 69–71.

Zegarowicz, E. J., *Inflation-Proof Your Future*, New York, Walker, 1971.

Index